The Winter Repertory
Michael Feingold / General Editor

the
winter repertory

2

María Irene Fornés
promenade
other & plays

INTRODUCTION: RICHARD GILMAN

WINTER HOUSE LTD

NEW YORK

To Mama Carmita

To Moira,

Fondly,

Gene

Feb. 23, '76

INTRODUCTION

In the spring of 1965 I directed María Irene Fornés' *Successful Life of 3* for the Open Theatre. The other members of the company and I had been unhappy with a production of the play that the group had done earlier, and felt in need of some principle of performance and presentation that would do justice to Miss Fornés' imagination and dramatic powers. And so I queried myself about just what kind of imagination she had and about her particular strengths as a playwright, and I thought I knew. She was "absurd," (the term was still new enough for you to think it told you something) blessed with a sense of the incongruities and discontinuities of language, zany, fruitfully illogical and tuned in to social inanity as a kind of radical parodist. All of which advanced textbook notions were of course entirely useless for knowing how to stage her work.

And then something happened during an early rehearsal, one of those windfalls which a director had better be able to recognize, that gave me the clue I needed. In the scene in the doctor's office at the beginning of the play, one of the men is ushered into an inner room; we assume he is seeing the doctor but learn, when he comes back, that he has "banged" the nurse who led him in. The script merely indicates that they return, but our actors came back instantly, which suggested that the act had been consummated with blinding, unheard-of speed. It struck us all as wonderfully funny and, more than that, as being exactly true to the way Irene Fornés organizes her stage time and, by extension, her stage space. Things happen outside chronologies and beyond known boundaries; the center of the action is sometimes in language, sometimes in gesture or sheer *mise-en-scène*, but always in a dimension unlocatable by any of our ordinary means of determining the whereabouts of what we consider truths.

This may be simply to say that Miss Fornés is a dramatist of almost pure imagination (as pure as imagination can be in an age of mixed media and life styles contending with those of art) whose interest in writing plays has little to do with making reports on what she's observed, in parodying society or behavior, or in "dramatizing" what already exists in the form of ordinary emotion or experience. But if this is a simple thing to say about her, it isn't any less important, because there are exceedingly few playwrights, particularly in America, of whom it can be said. Our genuine avant-garde is for the most part heavily implicated in the uses of the stage for therapy or social action, while our surrogate avant-garde goes on turning out its little "human" playlets about people who can't communicate, and so on.

In any case, we staged *Successful Life of 3* as a lucidly demented paradigm of human relationships, doing it as though it were a movie (Keaton, the Marx Brothers, the Keystone Kops: nothing to be imitated, but a spirit to assimilate) with the film's freedom precisely from the oppressions of finite time and space. We speeded up the action to a whirlwind pace, eliminating all the integuments, the texture of verisimilitude and logical connection which, to be sure, Miss Fornés had excluded as part of her principle of writing but which conventional theater wisdom would have put right back in. At other times we slowed things down to a crawl, violently exaggerating that emptiness, that duration in which nothing *active* happens, which the same received wisdom would have regarded as fatal to theatricality. In other words, we staged the play as it had been written, only we had to find out this manner for ourselves; like any true and confident artist, Miss Fornés doesn't tell you what she is doing, she does it.

Successful Life of 3 remains one of my favorites among Irene Fornés' works, along with *Dr. Kheal* and *A Vietnamese Wedding*. I admire to one major degree or another each of the other four plays in this volume—*Molly's Dream* and *The Red Burning Light* are especially interesting for the new density and range of the former and the surreal political intelligence of the latter—but the three works I mentioned above seem to me the essential products of Miss Fornés' dramatic imagination so far.

All three plays exhibit in very different ways her occupation of a domain strategically removed from our own not by extravagant fantasy but by a simplicity and matter-of-factness that are much more mysterious. *Successful Life of 3* organizes the "story" of a shifting triangle whose members behave much the way we do—once our behavior has been stripped of rationalizations. The play abstracts behavior patterns from ordinary life, removing the illusion of continuity, the sense of fitness which we too often suppose to be truth itself.

Dr. Kheal is an exercise in plausibility, a seeming parody of pedagogy but in fact a brilliant investigation of the myths of knowledge itself. Reminiscent (but by no means derivative) of the professor in Ionesco's *The Lesson*, its single character is a lecturer for whom "poetry is for the most part a waste of time, and so is politics . . . and history . . . and philosophy"—in short, everything sanctified—and who proceeds to offer a wholly new epistemology, logical, convincing, aggressive, far-seeing . . . and entirely unreal.

A Vietnamese Wedding is the play of Irene Fornés which least resembles conventional drama, even of a radical kind, yet it is also the quietest and seemingly most artless of all. Constructed in the form of a re-enactment of a traditional Vietnamese betrothal and marriage ceremony, it calls upon members of the audience to participate in its rites, without having to learn any roles or indeed to "act" at all, and upon the rest of the spectators to imagine themselves present at something historical and actual. Yet from this sober summons to reality, so lacking in the superficies of drama, we experience a strange displacement; in imitating an exotic social custom and limning it as though it were an actual event, we find ourselves in the very heart of the country of the dramatic. For theater is the imagining of possible worlds, not the imitation of real ones, and what could be more unreal to us than a ceremony like this play? In enacting it we learn not how other people live but how we are able to imagine ourselves as others, which is what drama is about. If María Irene Fornés had given us nothing else, it would be a remarkable thing to have accomplished. But of course she has given us much more.

Richard Gilman

A VIETNAMESE WEDDING

A Vietnamese Wedding was first enacted at Washington
Square Methodist Church in New York on February 4,
1967, as a part of the week-long cumulative protest against
American involvement in Vietnam called Angry Arts Week.
The following participated as readers:

Remy Charlip
María Irene Fornés
Aileen Passloff
Florence Tarlow

A subsequent series of enactments was given by the cast of
The Red Burning Light in connection with the
performances of that play at La MaMa Experimental
Theatre Club, beginning April 12, 1969.

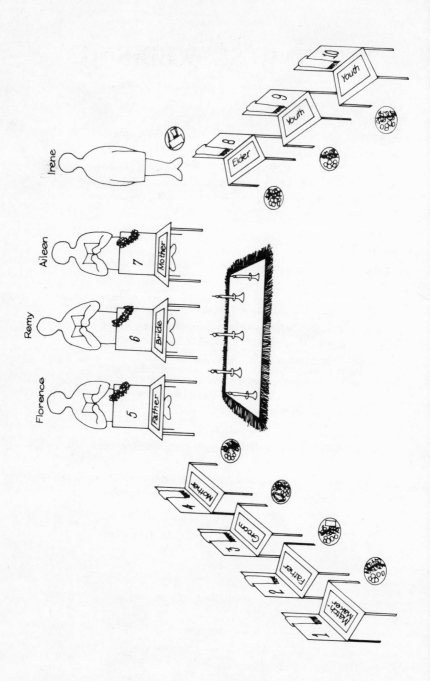

The following objects are to be set in the manner indicated in the diagram:

10 Chairs
10 5x7 cards
3 Flower garlands (about 24" around)
7 Red sashes (about 5' long)
8 Red trays or plates
Areca leaves (or a substitute)
Betel nuts (or a substitute)
1 Ring
1 Necklace
1 Bracelet
3 Bags of chocolate money
2 3x5 cards
1 Colorful floor mat
5 Candles and holders
1 Sheet of red rice paper
1 Match box
1 Pen
4 Whistles
4 Noisemakers
1 Tape of Vietnamese music (*Music of Vietnam*, Ethnic Folkways Library FE 4352, is suggested.)

The ten 5x7 cards will indicate the position of the participants and will be placed on the chairs as shown in the diagram.

The flower wreaths are to be placed on the back of chairs 5,6,7.

The red sashes are to be placed on the back of chairs 1,2,3, 4,8,9,10.

Seven trays are to be placed on the floor facing chairs 1,2,3, 4,8,9,10. They are to contain areca leaves and betel nuts. Besides these, the GROOM's tray will contain the ring, the necklace, and the bracelet; the FATHER OF THE GROOM's will contain the 3 chocolate money bags and a 3x5 card with the following speech:

Friends, neighbors, and
newly acquired family; may we take
your daughter to our house?

The second 3x5 card should have the following speech:

Friends, neighbors, and
newly acquired family; we allow you
to take our daughter to your house.

and should be held by FLORENCE.

The eighth red tray should be in a place accessible to IRENE, and
will contain the pen, the matches and the red rice paper with the
following message:

Rose Silk Thread God,
look after our marriage.

FLORENCE, REMY, AILEEN and IRENE will hold the whistles and
noisemakers and use them at the end of the piece.

A *Vietnamese Wedding* is not a play. Rehearsals should serve the
sole purpose of getting the readers acquainted with the text and
the actions of the piece. The four people conducting the piece
are hosts to the members of the audience who will enact the
wedding, and their behavior should be casual, gracious, and unob-
trusive.

FLORENCE, REMY, AILEEN, *and* IRENE *stand as indicated in the
diagram.*

REMY   We are going to present to you a Vietnamese wedding. And
we are going to ask a few of you to help us. What you have to
do is very simple. It doesn't require any acting ability, and we
will tell you what to do as we go along.
First, we'll choose the matchmaker.

REMY *chooses the members of the wedding party from the audience.* IRENE, FLORENCE, *and* AILEEN *help them to their seats, and help them put on their sashes around their waists and garlands on their heads.*

Then, we'll choose the father and the mother of the bride.
Then, the father and the mother of the groom.
Then, the groom.
Then, we choose the bride.
Now, the distinguished elder member of the groom's family.
And then, two young members of the groom's family.

FLORENCE, REMY, AILEEN, *and* IRENE *return to their positions.*

FLORENCE   In Vietnam, especially in the cities, there are young people who have rebelled against traditional customs. That is, they prefer to take it upon themselves to choose their own marital partner as they do in western countries. However, for the most part, Vietnamese youths follow tradition. Marriages are arranged by the parents with the aid of an experienced matchmaker. The matching of a pair is a complex and delicate matter. It requires the love and wisdom of parents, plus the objective judgment of a matchmaker. The bride and groom must be of equal social standing, equal education, and their moral history must also be equal.
Once the bride and groom are chosen according to these standards, their horoscopes are drawn. If the horoscopes indicate that their characters are not compatible or that there might be conflict between them at some point in their lives, another mate is chosen.

AILEEN   If a family is asked for their daughter or son in marriage, and they wish to refuse the offer without offending the suitor's family, they speak to the astrologer privately.

FLORENCE   If the offer is acceptable and the charts propitious, the wedding date is chosen.

REMY *(To the* BRIDE*)* When is your birthday?

The BRIDE *answers. To provide an example we will say* SHE *has answered May fifth.* REMY *then passes the information on to* FLORENCE.

May fifth.

FLORENCE *looks up the date in the accompanying chart and replies.*

January 1–20: Capricorn
January 21–31: Aquarius
February 1–19: Aquarius
February 20–28: Pisces
March 1–20: Pisces
March 21–31: Aries
April 1–19: Aries
April 20–30: Taurus
May 1–20: Taurus
May 21–31: Gemini
June 1–21: Gemini
June 22–30: Cancer
July 1–21: Cancer
July 22–31: Leo
August 1–21: Leo
August 22–31: Virgo
September 1–22: Virgo
September 23–30: Libra
October 1–22: Libra
October 23–31: Scorpio
November 1–21: Scorpio
November 22–30: Sagittarius
December 1–21: Sagittarius
December 22–31: Capricorn

FLORENCE   Taurus.

REMY   *(To the* GROOM*)* When is your birthday?

The GROOM *answers. We will say he was born November fifth.*

REMY *(To* FLORENCE*)* November fifth.

FLORENCE *looks up the date in the chart.*

FLORENCE Scorpio.

REMY Taurus and Scorpio. Very good!

AILEEN Very, very good!

FLORENCE Excellent!

REMY Formerly, girls were wed as young as thirteen and boys at sixteen. The reason for early marriages was usually economic. For some families, to give their daughter away meant one less mouth to feed. For others, to gain a daughter meant one more person to help with the housework. For some, the addition of a male meant another helping hand in the field. There was no general rule as to whether it was convenient to add or to subtract one number in the family. It depended on the particular needs of each household.
These early marriages were usually satisfactory to the family, but as the young people grew, it happened occasionally that they did not find their mate to their liking. A young woman tells us about her unhappy marriage in this popular poem:

AILEEN

> My mother was greedy.
> She wanted
> A basket of rice,
> A fat pig,
> And a Hang Kung tail.
>
> I asked her to refuse.
> But she said I was

Too young to know,
And brought me to my groom.

Now, I am fully grown.
I am tall and my husband is short.

We are like a pair of unequal chopsticks.

REMY   Child marriages are no longer common in Vietnam.

AILEEN   Though many things have changed, the wedding ritual remains the same. The betel nut and the areca leaf are symbolic of love and good will, and they are always exchanged as a most valuable offering between the bride's and the groom's families. The custom derives from an ancient myth.

FLORENCE   During the reign of Hung Wung III, there was a mandarin named Cao, who had two beautiful sons, Tan and Sung. One day, the mandarin and his wife died, and the two boys were left without a father, a mother, a house, or money. The boys had to go from town to town looking for work, and they could find none.
One day they came to the house of Magistrate Luu who happened to be a friend of their father Cao. Luu received the boys in his house, and said: "I never had a son and now I have two." It was true that Magistrate Luu didn't have a son, but he had a daughter who was as fair as a white lotus and as fresh as a spring rose. Naturally, both boys loved her the moment they saw her. But neither of them spoke to her of his love because each knew his brother also loved her.
Luu realized what was happening. He knew that the boys would become old and shriveled before they spoke to the maiden. To prevent that from happening, he decided he would follow the custom and give his daughter to the eldest. One day he said to Sung: "Which one of you is the eldest?" And Sung said: "Tan is the eldest," but Tan quickly said: "Sung is the eldest." Only one of them was telling the truth. But Luu, who was a very clever fellow, decided he would not ask any more questions. He knew

the boys would keep giving him the same answers. Instead, that night for dinner, he placed only one pair of chopsticks between the brothers.

When dinner was served, Sung, without giving it any thought, picked up the chopsticks and handed them to Tan. And Tan, without giving it any thought, received the chopsticks and bent down to eat, as any older brother would. "I found you out," said Luu to Tan. "You are the eldest. You will marry my daughter."

REMY Tan was now the happiest of men in all of Vietnam. He spent all his time taking walks with his new bride, reciting poetry to her, and singing love songs.

Sung overcame his love for the fair maiden and accepted his lot, for he wanted only joy and happiness for his beloved brother. But after a while, he realized that he was very lonely. He sat alone in his room waiting for a sign of care, or friendship, from Tan . . . but nothing happened.

In wild sorrow, he ran away from home, for he could stand the sadness no more. He ran and ran, passing leafy forests and flat meadows, until he reached the dark blue sea. Night came and Sung fell exhausted onto the ground, hungry and thirsty. His head was as hot as fire. And he cried and cried until he died and was turned into a white chalky rock.

When Tan realized his brother was gone, he went after him. He passed the leafy forests and the flat meadows and he arrived at the same dark blue sea. He too was exhausted. He sat down by the white chalky rock, and he cried and cried until he died. And he was turned into a tree with a straight stem and green palms. It was the areca tree.

AILEEN The lovely maiden missed her husband so much that she set off one day to look for him. She went along the same way as the brothers and reached the sea and lay down exhausted at the foot of the tall areca tree. Tears of despair rolled down her cheeks and she cried sorrowfully until she died. She was turned into a creeping plant—the betel—which twined around the lofty trunk of the areca tree.

That night, all the people in the village nearby had the same dream. They all dreamt the story of Tan, Sung and the maiden. The strange occurrence came to the ears of King Hung Wung III, who said: "If they were so devoted to each other, let us mix the three things, the rock, the areca leaf, and the betel nut, and see what happens." They burned the rock, which became white and soft, and they wrapped it in an areca leaf. Then they cut a piece of betel nut, and squeezed them all together. The mixture became liquid and red, like blood. The king then said: "This is the true symbol of conjugal and fraternal love. Let the tree and the plant be grown everywhere to remind us of true devotion and love. And let us chew the betel nut so that affection and good will will reign among us."

FLORENCE   The habitual chewing of the betel nut produces a blackening effect on the teeth, until they appear as though they have been lacquered. In the past, such black teeth were an object of admiration. A young man tells us about his loved one's teeth in a popular poem:

REMY

Do you remember me when you go home?
When I go home I remember your teeth.

I would pay one hundred taels
For your beautiful lips.

But for your black teeth
I would pay much more.

AILEEN   The wedding ceremony.

FLORENCE   The procedure is very formal. The date and hour must be exact, according to horoscopic readings. Everybody wears his best clothing. The boy's family wears red sashes around their waists.

REMY   The boy's family walks from the boy's home to the girl's home in a ceremonial procession.

IRENE *tells the members of the* GROOM*'s party to stand and pick up their trays.* SHE *leads them in a procession around the theater aisles, while* AILEEN *reads the following speech. The Vietnamese music is played softly.*

AILEEN   The matchmaker has previously discussed the amount and kind of gifts. As the gifts are to be distributed among the bride's family and friends, the larger the family the more gifts are required. If the groom's family is rich, the gifts will include sacks of grain, live animals, clothing, candles, incense, tea, cakes, betel nuts and areca leaves, but no matter how poor the family is, there will always be betel nuts and areca leaves.

FLORENCE   The gifts are placed on the ancestral altar by the groom's party.

IRENE *instructs the party to place the trays on the altar (floor mat). Then* SHE *instructs the* GROOM *and his* FATHER *to stand to the left of the altar, and* THE REST *to the right.*

REMY   The candles are lit.

IRENE *lights the candles with the help of some of the* GROOM*'s* FAMILY. *The music stops.*

AILEEN   The bridegroom gives the bride jewels—an engagement ring, a necklace and a bracelet.

If the GROOM *doesn't act of his own accord,* IRENE *will tell him what to do. The same applies to any of the following directions.*

FLORENCE   The father of the groom gives the bride, her father, and her mother a certain amount of money.

HE *does it.*

REMY   The groom's father makes a solemn request to take the bride away to their home.

The GROOM's FATHER *reads the card on his plate.*

Solemnly the father of the bride agrees.

FLORENCE *gives the* FATHER OF THE BRIDE *his card to read.* HE *reads it out loud.*

Then they all bow three times.

EVERYONE *bows three times.* IRENE *stands next to the* GROOM *with her tray.*

AILEEN   A message to the genie of marriage, the Rose Silk Thread God, is written on a red sheet of paper.

IRENE *gives the red paper to the* GROOM *to sign.*

Then, it is burned, so that the message will reach the genie.

The GROOM *burns the message.*

FLORENCE   They all bow three times again, paying their final respect to the genie.

EVERYONE *bows.*

REMY   At this point, the couple is considered married.

IRENE *tells the* GROOM *to take the* BRIDE *by the hand and head the procession.*

And a party is held with a lot of speechmaking, gift-giving, and merrymaking.

IRENE *leads the procession, going first around the* READERS, *then, along the aisles. The music starts softly while* REMY *reads.*

The groom's family traditionally acts as though they are very anxious to take the bride to their home. The groom's entourage then begins the trip home in the form of a procession with the bride and her attendants, friends, and relatives joining in. Little children sometimes set up roadblocks and ask tolls of the wedding party. These are readily paid, as they consider it bad luck to refuse.

FLORENCE   Upon arrival at the groom's house, the party is met by the loud noise of firecrackers.

The music plays loudly. FLORENCE, REMY, *and* AILEEN *join the procession, and blow their whistles.* IRENE *also blows her whistle and leads the procession out of the theater.*

THE RED BURNING LIGHT
Or: Mission XQ3

The Red Burning Light was first performed by the Open Theatre on their European tour in the summer of 1968. It was directed by Fredric de Boer and choreographed by James Barbosa, with the following cast:

The General   *Ron Faber*
Private Macoo   *Ralph Lee*
Private Lorodod   *Paul Zimet*
Private Lily   *Ellen Schindler*
General Fivestar   *Barbara Vann*
Ornithoptera Paradisea I   *Dorothy Lyman*
Ornithoptera Paradisea II   *Jayne Haynes*
Tenor   *James Barbosa*

A revised version of the play was subsequently performed at La MaMa E.T.C in New York, beginning on April 12, 1969. This production was directed by Remy Charlip, Ken Glickfeld, Messrs. de Boer and Barbosa, and the author, with music by Richard Peaslee and Jon Bauman, lighting by Paul Williams and John P. Dodd, and the same cast, except that James Barbosa played Private Lorodod. The version of *The Red Burning Light* published here incorporates the author's extensive revisions subsequent to the La MaMa production.

GENERAL: He wears an unkempt uniform. From his waist hangs a giant hypodermic needle. He carries a feather duster as a swagger stick.

PRIVATE MACOO: A simple young man. An elastic belt holds his very wide pants.

PRIVATE LORODOD: A poetic young man.

GENERAL FIVESTAR: A bosomy lady general. She also carries a swagger stick.

ORNITHOPTERA PARADISEA I: A butterfly with chiffon wings.

ORNITHOPTERA PARADISEA II: A butterfly with chiffon wings.

PRIVATE LILY: A sexy young lady. She wears a belted army shirt over khaki bikini panties.

KOOLY KOOLY: An Oriental.

INTERVIEWER: A television newscaster.

PRIVATE MACOO and KOOLY KOOLY are played by the same actor. PRIVATE LORODOD and THE INTERVIEWER are played by the same actor.

SCENE 1

A black curtain hangs between the proscenium and the back wall. Fancy colored lights flash on and off. There is a musical fanfare, and two light spots move around, creating a music-hall atmosphere. Both spots fall on the curtain midway between center and left. There is a loud cymbal crash. The GENERAL enters and bows. HE then does a parade march step to center; then moves back-

wards to left, then backwards to center, again triumphant. HE *repeats the same motions to the right.*

GENERAL   *(In the manner of a circus barker)* Ladies and gentlemen! We are going to present to you a great show.

Drum roll.

We were a hit in Asia.

Drum roll.

We were a hit in Africa.

Drum roll.

We were a hit all over the world.

Double drum roll.

And surely, we'll be a hit in our own home town too. Is it possible that we could be a hit in Asia, a hit in Africa, a hit all over the world, and not be a hit in our own home town? . . . Not a chance. Ladies and gentlemen, what we bring you tonight, on this stage, and in three-dimensional real life, is a step by step, in-depth presentation of the planning, development, and actual, exciting and thrilling execution of Mission XQ3. The mission that brought enlightenment, truth, peace, and, in one word, our message, around the world.

Drum roll.

Now you see why our success was absolute? Now you see why our success must be, has to be, will be, more than absolute here in our own home?

Drum roll.

Ladies and gentlemen, we've created a commotion wherever we've been. We've created an uproar, an upheaval. We've created riots, chaos, terror. . . . Ladies and gentlemen, I am proud to bring to you . . . the show . . . that leveled . . . the world!

Musical fanfare.

Ladies and gentlemen! The original cast!

While HE *speaks,* LILY, LORODOD, *and* ORNITHOPTERA PARADI-SEA I *enter from left.* FIVESTAR, MACOO *and* ORNITHOPTERA PARADISEA II *enter from right.* THEY *do a musical revue march.*

The original dramatis personae; the very same individuals who carried out the mission; themselves enacting their own roles. The mission and the show being one and the same. The heroes and the actors being one and the same. Ladies and gentlemen, *signori e signore, Damen und Herren* . . . direct from its triumphant, unprecedented, overwhelming success . . . The Red Burning Light, or Mission XQ3.

HE *joins the* OTHERS *in their march.*

ALL *(Singing)*

> Yeah yeah yeah yeah
> Yeah yeah yeah yeah
> This is the burning light
> Yeah yeah yeah yeah
> Of the American way of life
> Yeah yeah yeah yeah

THEY *line up and continue singing in a low voice through the following lines.*

GENERAL Attention men, present yourselves. The audience would like to know your names.

THEY *each step forward, salute and say their names while the* REST *march in place.*

MACOO   Private Macoo.

LORODOD   Private Lorodod.

FIVESTAR   General Fivestar.

ORNITHOPTERA PARADISEA I   Ornithoptera Paradisea.

ORNITHOPTERA PARADESEA II   Ornithoptera Paradisea.

LILY   Private Lily.

As SHE *salutes, her shirt opens and her breast is exposed. The* REST *stop singing.*

Oops, me titty's showing.

While THEY *sing,* THEY *march in front of* LILY, *who stands saluting.*

ALL

La la la la
Lala lala la la

LILY   Oops, me little titty's showing.

ALL

La la la la
Lala lala la la

LILY   Me little sweety titty's showing.

ALL

La la la la
Lala lala la la

LILY   Oops, me little sweety jumping jelly titty's showing!

GENERAL   Cover yourself up, Private Lily. Keep it clean. This is just
the introduction. And the introduction has got to be clean. *(As
HE sings, HE dusts the OTHERS with his duster)*

Keep it clean, Private Lily,
Keep it clean.
This is just the introduction,
And the introduction has got to be clean.
Cover your little titty, Private Lily.
The introduction has got to be clean.
Cover your little sweety titty, Private Lily.
Be a regular sort of guy.
Cover your little sweety jumping jelly titty,
Private Lily.
This introduction has got to be clean.

LILY   *(Covering herself)* Chucks.

GENERAL   Is everybody clean?

THEY *do bumps and grinds, scratch their asses, pick their noses
and burp; all line up,* GENERAL *last.*

ALL

La la la la
Lala lala la la
La la la la
Lala lala la la

GENERAL Wait a moment. Wait a moment. There's someone cheating here. This doesn't seem to work. *(HE moves in back of LILY)*

ALL

> La la la la
> Lala lala la la
> La la la la
> Lala lala la la

GENERAL Wait a moment. There's something crooked here. I'm just not getting the kicks that I should. *(HE moves in front of LILY)*

ALL

> La la la la
> Lala lala la la
> La la la la
> Lala lala la la

GENERAL Chucks and Schlitz! Nothing seems to work! Just as I suspected. There's a subvert in our midst. I have to investigate this here platoon, otherwise this mission will never be a success. Fall apart men, I have to get on with my work.

SCENE 2

The curtain rises. A backdrop depicts the GENERAL's office. Painted on the drop are: to the center, a large portrait of the GENERAL; on each side, an oval military emblem; below and to the sides of the portrait, two American flags. On each side and below the emblems are two doors. Under the portrait there is a chair looking somewhat like a throne on wheels. Hanging from the back of the chair are two magic wands, several rucksacks, fans, a pair of binoculars and a parasol. To the right of the chair

*is a large map with pushpins, and to the left, a stand with a
telephone. In front of the right side door, there is a trapdoor or
chute.*
The GENERAL *walks to his chair. The* REST *exit.* ALL *move their
hips in an exaggerated manner as* THEY *walk. The* GENERAL *sits
down, burps, scratches his back, burps again, scratches his buttocks, yawns, dusts himself, and combs his hair.* HE *is now ready
to start. The left door opens.* MACOO *stands on the threshold.*

GENERAL   In. *(To the audience)* Someone has knocked at the door.
And I've just told them to come in. *(*HE *waits)* In. *(*HE *waits)*
God damn it! Come in!

MACOO *marches in. The door closes behind him.*

MACOO   *(Saluting)* Ay ay ay, sir.

GENERAL   Come here, son. Stand here by me.

MACOO *stands by the* GENERAL *and salutes.*

MACOO   Ay ay ay, sir.

GENERAL   Take down your pants, Private Macoo. I want to see your
bare ass.

MACOO *starts tiptoeing away. The* GENERAL *grabs him by his
elastic belt. A siren sound accompanies the motion. The* GEN-
ERAL *speaks to the audience.*

We have to make sure that everyone is clean. *(*HE *looks down*
MACOO*'s pants, then, to the audience)* Where is it?

MACOO   You're looking at it, sir.

The GENERAL *bumps* MACOO *three times.*

Ay ay ay, sir!

GENERAL   Blasted Chrisanthemus! This ass just doesn't work. You need some medication. There's something wrong with you, young man.

The GENERAL *takes his hypodermic and gives* MACOO *a shot up his ass. A siren sound accompanies the motion.* MACOO *jumps up.*

MACOO   Ay ay ay!

GENERAL   I know what's wrong with you. You're sick in the head.

The GENERAL *hits* MACOO *on the head. Drum.*

There! You look better.

HE *looks* MACOO *over.*

Not really.

Putting his fist to MACOO*'s forehead and hitting his fist with the other hand. Drum.*

Here! You need a frontal lobotomy.

MACOO *babbles.*

Hm, that sounds very good. Let me try it now.

HE *jumps on* MACOO*'s back and rides him piggyback.* MACOO *collapses.*

I know what's wrong. You're doing it on purpose. He is sabotaging the works. I have to deal out swift justice. No more of that gentle-as-a-feather treatment.

HE *gives* MACOO *a blow, a kick, and another blow. Drum. Drum. Drum.*

You still don't look right to me. You look like an old banana peel. I'll make a man out of you yet. To the front with you, young man.

MACOO *starts exiting on his knees, shooting an imaginary rifle.*

The front? That reminds me of something. Hey, soldier, where's your front?

MACOO *thrusts his pelvis forward.*

MACOO   You're looking at it, sir.

The GENERAL *pulls* MACOO*'s pants at the waist and looks in.*

GENERAL   You call that zig-zag a kikkee? That looks nothing like the pictures I've seen. It's not even going in the right direction. To the front with you, young man. You need to be taught a thing or two.

MACOO *starts exiting on his knees, moving to the rhythm of the* GENERAL*'s words.*

If you want to know which way a kikkee goes you should take a look at mine. Back to front . . . front to back . . . left to right . . . right to left . . . up side down . . . down side up . . . It's where it should be . . . I'm sure of that.

MACOO *goes down the chute. The* GENERAL *walks to the chair, looking under one arm, then the other.* HE *sits down and burps.* HE *rises suddenly and speaks in the manner of a circus barker again.*

And now, ladies and gentlemen, we interrupt this fascinating drama to bring you the spectacular dancing butterflies. . . . Ladies and gentlemen . . . *Ornithopterae Paradiseae.*

The music to "Poor Butterfly" starts. ORNITHOPTERA PARADISEA
I *and* II *enter as the* GENERAL *exits.* THEY *do a lyrical dance and
exit. The* GENERAL *enters applauding.*

GENERAL   Ladies and gentlemen . . . *Ornithopterae Paradiseae* . . .

ORNITHOPTERA PARADISEA I *and* II *re-enter and bow.* THEY *exit.
The* GENERAL *goes to his chair and burps. The telephone rings.
The* GENERAL *picks it up.*

Grr. *(Pause)* Grr. *(Pause)* Grr.

HE *hangs up, goes to the map and changes the position of a pin.*
HE *goes to his chair and burps. The left door opens.* LORODOD
and LILY *stand on the threshold.* LORODOD *puts a gas mask on*
LILY.

LORODOD   Lily, love, fear not, you look fine.

LILY *wiggles.*

He'll never know you are a girl, Lily love. You are perfectly
disguised.

LILY *nods.*

Just don't show him your titty, Lily dear. Please, do keep yourself
covered.

LILY *nods.*

Remember, Lily love, if you keep your titty covered, we'll be
forever together. But if you show your titty, they'll keep us apart.
Do you understand?

LILY *nods.* LORODOD *and* LILY *march downstage and salute.
When* LILY *salutes, her breast is exposed.*

LILY   Oops, me little ti . . .

> LORODOD *covers* LILY*'s mouth with one hand and fixes her shirt with the other.*

GENERAL   What's that?

LORODOD   What, sir?

GENERAL   *(Pointing to* LILY*)* That.

LORODOD   That's Private Lily, sir.

GENERAL   What's wrong with him?

LORODOD   Nothing, sir.

GENERAL   I think Private Lily needs some exercise. He looks infirm to me.

LORODOD   He's not, sir. He's petite. They come that way some times.

GENERAL   I need men with a big fighting spirit, a high morale. I need to make a good impression. This Private Lily looks like a mishap.

LORODOD   He's a good soldier, sir.

GENERAL   He looks like he belongs in the Navy, with those them there big eyes and those protruding lips. Let's see you do one hundred and fifty push-ups, Private Lily. Let's see you do that.

> LILY *goes on her hands and knees and starts pushing up and down.* LORODOD *tries to help her get in the right position.*

Do your push-ups, Private Lily, you dumb yo-yo.

> HE *rides* LILY.

LILY   *(Enjoying the* GENERAL*)* Oh . . .

GENERAL   Jumping Chrisanthemus, Lily. You wiggle like a jelly pot.

LORODOD   He's a fine soldier, sir. He wiggles because he must.

The GENERAL *feels* LILY*'s biceps.*

GENERAL   Not much muscle here. I'll have to send him back to basic training. *(*HE *reaches* LILY*'s breast)* My mistake. I feel a good biceps here. Yes, indeed, this biceps is as good as any biceps I ever got hold of. Oh, boy, what a biceps. Yum. Yum. Yes, sir, this biceps is a jewel, a general gem. *(*HE *yodels as* HE *holds* LILY*'s breast)* Yodoloodoloodoloo . . . *(Singing)*

> Yes, this biceps
> Feels like no biceps
> I ever felt.
> Point the way,
> Private Lily,
> Point the way.
> Fly away,
> Take me to battle.
> Fly away.
> Fly fly fly flyfly awayyyyy.

LILY *collapses. The* GENERAL *still sits on her.*

Chucks and Schlitz. This damn horse is not getting me anywhere. I thought it would make me fly but it didn't. *(*HE *is crestfallen)* For a moment I thought I had it. Yodoloodoloodoloo . . . But I didn't.

LORODOD   You just don't have your heart in it, sir.

GENERAL   Ah, true, true. There is only one thing I am interested in, and that is war. All my life I have wanted to lead men in desperate battle, but Private Lily won't help. *(Singing)*

Move on Private Lily
To battle I go
I go IgoIgoIgoIgo
To battle I goooooooo.

LILY *takes off her mask.*

LILY   Oh, get off me, General. You twiddle like an old balloon. You dumb flute.

The GENERAL *is suddenly surprised. Then* HE *gives* LORODOD *a knowing look, and signals him to get closer.*

GENERAL   Private, *this* is a girl.

LORODOD   Oh, no sir, she's a guy. She's in the army.

GENERAL   Nope, she's a girl. I can tell by her voice. (HE *points upward)* It's high.

LORODOD   Oh, no, sir, it's low.

GENERAL   No, it's high. Private Lily, speak.

LILY *makes growling sounds.*

How does that sound?

LORODOD   It sounds low.

GENERAL   Speak again, Lily.

LILY *repeats the growling sounds.*

My mistake. It does sound low. I guess Private Lily's a regular sort of guy.

GENERAL AND LORODOD   *(Singing)*

Oh, yes, Private Lily
's a regular sort of guy.
Oh, yes, Private Lily
Moves like a tank.
Oh, yes, Private Lily
Smokes a pipe.
Oh, yes, Private Lily
Can wallop a champ.
Oh, yes. Oh, yes.
Oh, yes, Private Lily
's a regular sort of guy.

GENERAL   Let me be the first to congratulate you men. You have just
joined Mission XQ3.

The THREE *form a line, pelvis to buttocks.*

Oh, yes. Oh, yes.
Oh, yes. Oh, yes.
Oh, yes, Private Lily
's a regular sort of guy
Oh, yes, Private Lily
Can wallop a champ.

There is a musical fanfare. The door to the right opens. GENERAL
FIVESTAR *enters.*

FIVESTAR   There! I caught you. If I had a camera, I'd take a snap.
But no matter, I have a photographic memory. One, two, three;
the girl in the front; the Private in the back; the General in the
middle. All moving in a lewd manner. There, I have it all printed
in my mind. The General is lucky Pierre. I'll report you to the
higher Archies. And in the meantime I'll join the conga line.
*(*SHE *joins the line)*

LILY   Who's that?

FIVESTAR   General Fivestar of the infantry.

GENERAL   Well, I'm afraid you came in the wrong door, and out you go. *This* is not the infantry.

FIVESTAR   It will be as soon as I send you awalking, General Kikkeelost.

GENERAL   Kikkeelost yourself. I know where my kikkee is. Show me your kikkee, and I'll show you mine. Ha ha. There! I caught you.

FIVESTAR   You caught what? You dumb kikkee. You never caught anything in your life. I'm General Fivestar come to join Mission XQ3. *(Pointing to her medals)* And here is my credentials. *(The* GENERAL *looks very closely at* FIVESTAR*'s bosom)*

GENERAL   Jumping Chrisanthemus! You're a woman general.

FIVESTAR   Are you kidding?

GENERAL   No. I'm not kidding. You're a woman general. I can tell by your posture.

FIVESTAR   What posture?

GENERAL   *(Pulling his shirt on his chest)* This posture. Women always have a hump in the front.

FIVESTAR   There's nothing wrong with my posture, you mentally retarded cretin.

SHE *hits him on the head. Drum.*

These here things you see on my chest are no hump. They're boobs.

GENERAL   Them there things might be boobs, but they're also a hump. Perhaps they're a boob-hump, but they sure are a hump.

FIVESTAR *hits the* GENERAL *on the head. Drum.*

FIVESTAR   I'll give you a hump in the head. You mentally retarded cretin. You're a shame to the Academy and the country for which you stand. Put him in the morgue. We don't need a sickening critter like you around here. Wrap him up in a bundle and feed him to the worms. He's the shame of the nation. Don't know the difference between them here boobs and a hump. I'm taking over this here platoon and all its barracks, and I'm making myself a six-star general. Take him to the dump.

LORODOD *picks up the* GENERAL *by the shoulders;* LILY, *by the feet. The door to the right opens.* ORNITHOPTERA PARADISEA I *and* II *enter carrying* MACOO *by the shoulders and feet.*

What bringest thou here, sisters?

ORNITHOPTERA PARADISEA I   *(Reciting)*

We found this soldier
Marching on his knees.
Why, Cinquestelli,
Was this soldier
Marching on his knees?

ORNITHOPTERA PARADISEA II

Why, oh why is there
So much woe
In the world?

FIVESTAR   Who knows. *(To* LILY *and* LORODOD*)* Take him to the dump.

ORNITHOPTERA PARADISEA I *and* II *put* MACOO *down and comfort him.*

GENERAL Jumping Chrisanthemus, General. From this angle you look precious.

FIVESTAR Precious?

GENERAL Rich.

FIVESTAR Rich?

GENERAL You look divine, madam. You look effervescent and clean. Star brilliantis. Succulent bloom. I love you.

FIVESTAR *(Feigning indifference)* . . . You don't love me . . .

GENERAL Yes, I do, madam. Tell these soldatis to put me down, and I'll show you. I can't wait to get at you.

FIVESTAR *(Rolling her eyes)* . . . Liar . . .

GENERAL Oh, star, give me a kiss . . . a kiss? . . . Why did I never think of that? Give me a kiss.

FIVESTAR Release him.

THEY *release him.* HE *goes to her on his knees and recites, exaggerating the "W" sounds.*

GENERAL

Madam, before my eyes laid on you,
I wailed like a waif,
I wallowed in woe,
I was wan.

But oh, you witch,
Since the first time I saw you,

I am wacky,
I wake with a whoop.
Woow! Woow!
I feel like a wolf.
I am woozy.

Madam, it's your whammy.
I whirl on your way like a windmill.
I am wayward,
I am walleyed,
I am wanton,
Madam, I'm won by your wiggle.

How's that?

FIVESTAR   I like it . . . it shows effort.

GENERAL

Oh, Star, Star, Star,
Princess enormous.
Oh, Star, military dream.
Oh, Star, give me a kiss.
Love of my life,
Give me a kiss.

HE *is still on his knees.* SHE *bends down and kisses him. Only
their lips touch.* HE *yodels and faints.* SHE *puts one foot on him
and raises her arms.* ORNITHOPTERA PARADISEA I *and* II *do a brief
dance with magic wands.*

ORNITHOPTERA PARADISEA I AND II   (*Reciting*)

And so did love triumph.
And so did love reign.
Kikkeelost was overwhelmed
By my sister Cinquestelli
Sent from above
So two tyrants

Could love.
Kikkeelost has Cinquestelli;
Cinquestelli, Kikkeelost.
Lorodod has his Lily,
And Lily her Lorodod,
But who do the Ornies have?

MACOO *tiptoes behind them and puts his arms around them.*

MACOO   Me.

ORNITHOPTERA PARADISEA I   Oh.

ORNITHOPTERA PARADISEA II   Oops.

THEY *run off flirtatiously.* HE *catches them, and* THEY *run off again.* THEY *step over the* GENERAL. HE *sits up and waves his arms as if to chase flies.* MACOO *catches* ORNITHOPTERA PARADISEA I. ORNITHOPTERA PARADISEA II *offers him her hand from a distance.* MACOO *stretches his arm toward her.* THEY *giggle and scream.* MACOO *catches* ORNITHOPTERA PARADISEA II *and* ORNITHOPTERA PARADISEA I *escapes.* THEY *run around some more until* HE *catches them both.*

ORNITHOPTERA PARADISEA I AND II   Oops, Mr. Macoo.

HE *kisses them.* THEY *sigh deeply.*

And we too have our gift
From the heavens above.

THEY *flutter. The* GENERAL *waves his hands.*

GENERAL   What's all this verming coming in here for? Get the insecticide, men. I've been getting some bedbugs and lice, but these giant flies is a bad sign.

FIVESTAR   *(Hitting the* GENERAL *on the head)* Them there vermin is not flies, you dumb flock. They is butterflies. Ornithopterae

Paradiseae to be exact. Curtsey for the General, girls, and show him how you can be ladylike.

THEY *curtsey. The* GENERAL *looks at them with disgust.*

These here Ornithopterae are my aides. They are in the infantry too, so treat them with respect. Curtsey for the General, girls.

THEY *curtsey.*

GENERAL   Grrr.

FIVESTAR   No need to act like the beast that you are, General.

ORNITHOPTERA PARADISEA I AND II   No need.

LORODOD   A need there is, but not a reason.

FIVESTAR *and the* GENERAL *look at* LORODOD, *surprised.*

GENERAL   That's right, Private. You tell them. All right. Is everybody ready?

ALL   Ready.

GENERAL   Stand up straight. We have this here image abroad that we have to maintain. It looks something like this.

HE *crosses his eyes, sticks his tongue out, makes claws with his hands, and bends his knees.* THEY ALL *imitate him.*

Yeah. But keep your backs straight.

THEY *straighten their backs.*

That's better. Every man and thing get your rucksacks and away we go, chipper and bright. Away away away away we go. Let's go, madam, we'll conquer the universe.

The GENERAL *takes* FIVESTAR *by the hand, turns her under his arm and starts pushing the chair in front of him.* HE *gets the binoculars and hangs them around his neck.* ORNITHOPTERA PARADISEA I *gets the parasol. The* REST *get rucksacks and fans.* THEY *line up behind the* GENERAL *and walk around the stage in time to music.*

SCENE 3

While THEY *march, a backdrop depicting a tropical landscape is lowered. The green leafage is held up in such a manner that when released it will flop down, exposing the reverse side.* THEY *begin to get tired and slow down.* FIVESTAR *collapses on the chair. The* GENERAL *sits on the arm of the chair. The* REST *collapse around them. The heat is intense.* THEY *fan themselves and wipe their foreheads.*

GENERAL   A tiring trip. Our Colonies of the East are further than we thought.

FIVESTAR   Sit on my lap, General. You'll feel the comfort of my charisma.

The GENERAL *sits on her lap and puts his head on her breast.*

Isn't it true that a woman's bosom brings comfort to a man?

GENERAL   It does, but I have to run and inflict our presence on the natives. We have been here for three seconds and we must waste no more time. Come with me, Private Lorodod, let's lay down our message. Toodle-oo, my love.

FIVESTAR   Toodle-oo.

SHE *looks around. The* GENERAL *exits moving his hips in an exaggerated manner.* LORODOD *follows him.*

Go fetch us a waiter, Private Macoo.

HE *starts to go and stops.*

We're dying of thirst. The heat in the tropics is just as they have it in the jungle movies back home . . . seething. . . . A true depiction. Write that down, Private Lily, make a note of it. You'll be our secretary. Make a note of everything the General and I say. We're full of wisdom and it shouldn't go to waste. And write it down neatly, we want to impress the folks back home who don't know how these expeditions are carried on.

LILY *takes out pad and pencil.* FIVESTAR *dictates.*

"True depiction in movies back home. The jungle is indeed hot. Seething to be more precise." I give it to you plain as a form of shorthand. You make it flowery and good, that's how come you're the scribe.—Fetch us a waiter, Private Macoo,

MACOO *starts to go and stops.*

and tell him we're dying of thirst. Tell him to bring us a round of Kool-Aid . . . pink . . . pink Kool-Aid all around, pineapple. How's that?

ORNITHOPTERA PARADISEA I   Fine.

ORNITHOPTERA PARADISEA II   Good.

LILY   Sure.

MACOO   Aye, aye, madam.

Not knowing which way to go, MACOO *goes around in circles for a while.* ORNITHOPTERA PARADISEA I *and* II *follow him, fluttering.* HE *disappears and* THEY *wave to him.*

ORNITHOPTERA PARADISEA I AND II   *(Plaintively)* Macoo . . . Macoo.

FIVESTAR   Did you notice what I noticed? He no longer says "Ay ay ay, madam" which used to reflect his pain . . . Now he just says "Aye aye" which is how it should be, and I know the reason too. Ask me what the reason is.

ORNITHOPTERA PARADISEA II   What is the reason?

ORNITHOPTERA PARADISEA I and II sit with their backs to the audience, holding up the parasol.

FIVESTAR   The reason is that he is in love. That is the reason. Let that be a lesson to you all. Love is a good cure for pain, and that is what we have to teach the world. Make a note of that, Private Lily. That is what we have to teach the world.

There is the sound of a bomb, ending with a sound somewhat like a toilet flushing. Part of the green leafage is released exposing ash and burnt-colored leaves. Small amounts of smoke are released in various places. FIVESTAR *puts her hand to her ear to identify the sound.*

Get your rucksacks ready, men, I believe our duty's dung.

The GENERAL *and* LORODOD *enter marching. The* GENERAL *wears new medals on his chest.* LORODOD *is crosseyed and wobbly.*

GENERAL   Hup hup one two stop.

THEY *come to a stop. The* GENERAL *salutes.*

Mission accomplished my little butterfly. *(Making his medals tinkle)* This is what I got for the boomboom. I got all this.

ALL

Boom
Boomboom Boomboom Boomboom
Boom Boom

Boom
Boomboom Boomboom Boomboom
Boom Boom
We got some medals
For the Boomboom.

The GENERAL *sits on the chair. The* INTERVIEWER *goes on one knee next to him. The* REST *stand around the* GENERAL, *making a family portrait.*

GENERAL   Well, it wasn't always as easy as that. You see, there were places where we couldn't shoot right away. No . . . we had to be more diplomatic. Yes, in places like that we had a harder time.

INTERVIEWER   Like for instance, sir?

GENERAL   Like for instance there was a particular place where we had instructions not to shoot right away and we went in there and the natives wanted to play games with us.

INTERVIEWER   What games?

GENERAL   Well, they made the missus here queen for a day.

INTERVIEWER   That sounds good, sir.

GENERAL   Yes, it sounds good but it wasn't. They wanted to play this game they call "This Is Your Life."

INTERVIEWER   I know that game.

GENERAL   You do?

INTERVIEWER   Yes.

GENERAL   Well, it's a mean game.

INTERVIEWER   It is?

GENERAL   Yes, they were going to roast us. That was the game.

INTERVIEWER   Oh.

GENERAL   Yes . . . and I said to them, "What do you mean this is my life?" I was trying to dissuade them. And they said, "Never you mind what we mean." And I said: "It isn't that I mind," (I was being diplomatic) I said, "It isn't that I mind, but why don't you play a different game?" And they said, "Hakashanaki hashaka." Which means . . .

The GENERAL *moves his lips and the* INTERVIEWER *blips.*

At which point I said, "Why do you have to roast the whole lot of us? The missus here and I are unsavory and tough. Why don't you just roast the butterflies. In my part of the world they are a delicacy. Ornithroptera Paradisea au gratin." I was lying of course, anything to save the skin. And then, they said in their particular kind of tongue, "Not enough meat." Then, I tried to talk them into cooking Private Macoo here. I was talking to them about his culinary advantages when they said they were going to cook whoever they pleased and they didn't need my advice. I said, "Well, but I am a very renowned chef. I even have my own television program. Private Macoo would make a very good fondue." At that point they sent for the hikinai. That's a seventeen-inch hatchet with a cat-o-nine-tails strung up at the end in case they miss.

INTERVIEWER   Holy smoke!

GENERAL   Yes . . . they were going to chop us up with that and then cook us. Then they started saying the hikinai prayer, and I said, "You know, that isn't kosher." I was trying to get them with a religious bit. It didn't do any good. They started saying their prayer and lo and behold we got away.

INTERVIEWER   How?

GENERAL   We had the means.

INTERVIEWER   And what was that?

GENERAL   Well, they have to close their eyes before they say the hikinai prayer. You see, if they don't close their eyes, it doesn't work. And that's when we got away, when they closed their eyes.

INTERVIEWER   And didn't they come after you?

GENERAL   No . . . we had the hikinai.

INTERVIEWER   Gosh . . .

MACOO *enters with a smoking coconut.* HE *kneels next to* FIVE-STAR *and offers it to her.* FIVESTAR *looks at it.*

GENERAL   A kiss, melove. I'm going to drop another boomboom.

SHE *gives him a kiss.*

No need to come. I can do it all alone.

HE *exits, hopping from foot to foot.*

FIVESTAR   What's that?

MACOO   Pink Pineapple.

FIVESTAR   Take it back. Tell them we want our money back.

MACOO *starts to go and stops.*

Pink pineapple indeed. Wrapped in what? It looks like horse manure. Tell them at home we wrap Kool-Aid in plastic envelopes. Write this down, Private Lily. "In the Orient they wrap Kool-Aid in horse manure." Take it back, Private Macoo.

MACOO *starts to go and stops.*

Fools we are but not to that degree. True or false? Answer, someone, true or false?

LILY   True.

MACOO   . . . False . . .

LORODOD   Yes.

FIVESTAR   What do you think, butterfly, true or false?

ORNITHOPTERA PARADISEA I *and* II *do not answer.*

Butterflies, you there butterflies . . .

ORNITHOPTERA PARADISEA I   I prefer to answer by my given name, not by my species.

ORNITHOPTERA PARADISEA II   Do I call you woman, or Cinquestelli?

FIVESTAR   Well, then, Ornithoptera Paradisea, what do you think? *(Aside)* Can you blame me for not being precise? If my name were Ornithoptera Paradisea I'd change it.

ORNITHOPTERA PARADISEA II   Indeed.

ORNITHOPTERA PARADISEA I   Likewise, madam.

FIVESTAR   One true, one false, one yes, indeed, and one likewise. Fortunately I have forgotten the question, and I'm sure none of these cretins remembers it either. Otherwise we would now be in the midst of the first disagreement of this our democratic caravan of love. Take the drink back, Private Macoo, and tell them they have some nerve.

MACOO *exits.*

This place is a dump and the service is atrocious. Take that down, Private Lily. "The place is a dump and the service is atrocious." Next time we skip this dump.

There is the sound of a bomb as before. The rest of the leaves fall. There is more smoke. FIVESTAR *puts her hand to her ear.*

That's boomboom number two.

The GENERAL *enters holding a Napolenic pose.* HE *takes long strides.*

GENERAL   Madam, I did it again.

FIVESTAR   Good show, my little boomboomleeboom.

GENERAL   *(Offering her his arm)* Come, let me show you what I've done.

THEY *walk leisurely and disappear behind the trees.* LORODOD *and* LILY *stand close together, so do* ORNITHOPTERA PARADISEA I *and* II.

LORODOD   *(Singing)*

My darling,
Have you noticed how strangely
The sun submerges beyond the land?
"The Sunset."
It is strange.

The sun is, as usual, pink, purple, and subtle,
But the land does not provide
The usual embroidered outline,
"Landscape."
It is flat.

Nor does the land contribute to the colors
Of the scheme its usual verdure.
"Foliage."
It is gray.

Have you noticed how the substance
We stand on,
"Soil,"
Is brittle?

And that breathing is rather hard,
"Difficult?"
The air is dry.

The GENERAL *and* FIVESTAR *return from the left.* KOOLY KOOLY
enters right. HE *is played by the same actor as* MACOO. HE *wears
an old, torn smock.* HE *holds the sides of his eyes back.* HE *stands
motionless facing front till* HE *exits.*

GENERAL   Well, what do you know, here's a native, my love. He
seems to have survived the boomboom.

FIVESTAR   Well, you finally came. Pink Kool-Aid for everyone, pineapple. That's one, two, three, four, five, six, seven.

LORODOD   Madam, pineapple is not pink.

FIVESTAR   Why not?

LORODOD   It isn't, madam. It never was.

GENERAL   She wants pineapple, not any old color pineapple, but
pink. Right, my love?

FIVESTAR   Right.

GENERAL   Tell the waiter what you want, my one.

FIVESTAR   Pink Pineapple.

GENERAL   On the double. One two three and off you go. He seems
to be transfixed, my love. Have you been making eyes at him?
. . . I kid, I kid. I know you're true to me. Preach to him, my
darling, tell him how love conquers all pain.

FIVESTAR   I want a whole lot of people to preach to, not just one
crummy jink.

GENERAL   Oh.

FIVESTAR   I want a crowd.

GENERAL   *(To* KOOLY KOOLY*)* Go get a crowd. Rally up your men.
The missus would like to speak to you. Go, go, move.

KOOLY KOOLY   *(Singing, in a green spot light)*

I coom flom li del
To tell woo woo yell pay
Yool skin ill be toln flom yool boly
And yul ees ill be peerce and fol flum
Deil sodet.

And yul lims ill be pooty of blud and bown
As main wer.
Ha ha ha. Ha ha ha. Ha ha ha.
Yool ill pay, if not heel in lel.

The lights begin to go back to normal.

LORODOD   Sir, that was a beautiful song. Would you write the words
down? My friend Lily and I like to harmonize and we would like
to add your song to our repertory.

ORNITHOPTERA PARADISEA I   I also sing and harmonize. And so does
my friend, Orni.

ORNITHOPTERA PARADISEA II   We would, if we may, like to join you.

LORODOD *sings a note.* ORNITHOPTERA PARADISEA I *and* II *do harmony to it.*

LORODOD   Lily, since you are the scribe, you write the words down.

THEY *stand in a circle around* KOOLY KOOLY.

KOOLY KOOLY

I coom flom li del
To tell woo woo yeel pay.
Yool skin ill be toln flom yool boly
And yul ees ill be peerce and fol flum
Deil sodet.

And yul lims ill be pooty of blud and bown
As main wer.
Ha ha ha. Ha ha ha. Ha ha ha.
Yool ill pay, if not heel in lel.

GENERAL   Fine, fine, give him a candy bar to show our appreciation.

LORODOD *takes out a candy bar.*

Shove it down his throat so he knows what to do with it.

LORODOD *opens* KOOLY KOOLY *'s mouth and shoves the candy bar down his throat. Then,* LORODOD *looks cross-eyed and shakes.*

Good, good, that's the spirit of brotherhood. He doesn't understand anything we say. Just smile to him so he knows we're
friendly.

The REST *smile.*

Give him a kick in the ass so he gets out of the way.

HE *gives* KOOLY KOOLY *a kick.*

We have to use the runway. Good-bye. Good-bye. Up up up and away we go. Get the sails up, men, we travel by sea this time.

THEY *form a boat.* LILY *is the masthead.* ORNITHOPTERA PARADISEA I *and* II *are the sails.* KOOLY KOOLY *disappears behind the trees. The boat moves as* THEY *sing in a cheerful rhythm. A backdrop depicting a blue sky is lowered.*

ALL

I come from the dead
To tell you you will pay.
Your skin will be torn from your body,
And your eyes will be pierced,
And fall from their sockets.

And your limbs will be putty of blood and bones.
As mine were.
Ha ha ha. Ha ha ha. Ha ha ha.
You will pay, if not here, in hell.

MACOO *runs in and climbs on the boat.*

GENERAL   Climb on board and sing our song, private Macoo. We have a new tune. Sails ahoy. Up up and away we go.

THEY *are in high sea. The* GENERAL *stands leaning his groin on* LILY*'s buttocks.* THEY *move with the swaying of the boat.* FIVE-STAR *and* LORODOD *look out to sea.*

MACOO   Now, Lily, you are a one-man woman and you shouldn't be doing that. You shouldn't be a many-man woman. There are enough many-man women, and not enough one-man women. I like you the way you are, Lily, and I don't want you to change.

ORNITHOPTERA PARADISEA I   I like you the way you are too, Lily, and
I don't want you to change either.

ORNITHOPTERA PARADISEA II   There are already too many many-man
women.

MACOO   Yes, Lily.

LILY   *(Moving away from the* GENERAL*)* Nuts!

MACOO   I am a two-woman man, Lily. But there's nothing wrong
with that. That doesn't mean that I am a man-women man, just
two.

ORNITHOPTERA PARADISEA II   Yes, Lily, he's right. I am a two-women
man. . . . No . . . I am a one-man two-women.

ORNITHOPTERA PARADISEA I   No, Orni, we're a half of a two-woman-
man woman.

ORNITHOPTERA PARADISEA II   No, Orni, we are a half-man woman.

ORNITHOPTERA PARADISEA I   No, Orni, we're a two-women-man
woman.

ORNITHOPTERA PARADISEA II   I think you're right, Orni.

ORNITHOPTERA PARADISEA I   Yes, Orni, that's what we are.

MACOO   Yes, Lily. You see?

The GENERAL *looks through the binoculars. A film of African
natives coming toward the boat in canoes is projected on the back
wall. The outline of the projection is like that of binoculars. The*
GENERAL *turns to talk to the* OTHERS *and the projection disappears.*

GENERAL   Get the boomboom ready. They must have heard we're
coming.

HE *looks through the binoculars again. The film is seen again. The* REST *go through the motions of loading a gun.*

Artillery, this is XQ3. Request a fire mission.

LORODOD   Roger. Send it.

GENERAL   Grid 348978. Proximity of friendlies, five feet. Azimuth.

LORODOD   What will it be?

GENERAL   Battery six.

There is the sound of a bomb as before. THEY *move as if the boat is rocking. The film shows an explosion. Then an empty shore.*

That was a big kill count. All right, men, stand up straight. We're going to be landing shortly.

THEY *fix their clothes and pose for the landing.*

LORODOD   Lily, dear, your cap is crooked.

GENERAL   *(Still posing)* Listen, Private, we won't have any of that around here.

LORODOD   What, sir?

GENERAL   That "Lily dear" and "Lily love." In the army we call men private, not love.

LORODOD   Yes, sir.

GENERAL   Jumping Chrisanthemus, Star, you look resplendent.

FIVESTAR   Just leave me a crowd to preach to. You blow them up before I get to preach to them.

GENERAL   Roger.

THEY *move back and forth suggesting the boat hitting sand. The sky drop is lifted, exposing the green tropical landscape.* THEY ALL *step off the boat, walk toward the trees and disappear behind them, to the accompaniment of a royal march. The stage is empty for a while, while the music plays.* FIVESTAR*'s voice is then heard in the distance over the music. Her words are undistinguishable. There is the sound of a bomb as before. The leaves drop, showing the burnt side and there are small amounts of smoke in various places. There is silence for a moment and the royal march starts again.* THEY ALL *enter, walk toward the spot where* THEY *left the boat, form the boat again and start singing.*

ALL

I come from the dead
To tell you you will pay.
Your skin will be torn from your body,
And your eyes will be pierced,
And fall from their sockets.

The GENERAL *and* FIVESTAR *promenade up and down the stage through the following speech.* HE *speaks in a soft romantic tone.*

GENERAL   Spying? Yes, we do our bit of spying here and there. But we don't call it that. . . . We call it intelligence, that fine thing. . . . Disarmament? Indeed . . . oh, beautiful thing . . . I'm all for it. . . . Arm—disarm same thing. War—peace, same thing. . . . One leads to the other and vice-versa. Rigmarole and abracadabra, same thing. All on our side though.—The armed fist with a tight grip on lightning . . . and the laurel leaf. Peace is our profession, madam. And that is our emblem . . . with the hand raised up to the sky and the clouds soaring by.—Yes, peace is our profession. Open Sesame and there you are; from the beginning to the end peace and freedom . . . you understand? *(Taking her to the chair)* Sure, my love, that was a nice prome-nade . . . cool and calm. Yes. It's all here in the book. *(Coming*

forward with the book) Ladies and gentlemen, *Operation XQ3.*
Take advantage of this special offer now. If this explosive book
does not bludgeon your mind send it back within fifteen days
and you will get your money back. Read all of the gory details.
And if you send for the book now. Listen to this; if you send for
the book now, you will get *free of charge* a weekly supplement
informing you of the progress and exciting activities of Mission
XQ3. Ladies and gentlemen, XQ3 is on the job. XQ3 lives. The
boomboom goes on.

ALL

Boom
Boomboom Boomboom Boomboom
Boom Boom
Boom
Boomboom Boomboom Boomboom
Boom Boom

*Films of small towns and cities being bombarded cover the
screen.*

Boom
Boomboom Boomboom Boomboom
Boom Boom

GENERAL *(Looking through the binoculars)* Artillery, XQ3 request
fire mission.

Bomb.

ALL

Boom
Boomboom Boomboom Boomboom
Boom Boom

GENERAL   Grid 38383. Azimuth.

Bomb.

ALL

Boom
Boomboom Boomboom Boomboom
Boom Boom

*The stage darkens gradually and the sounds become progressively
more faint.*

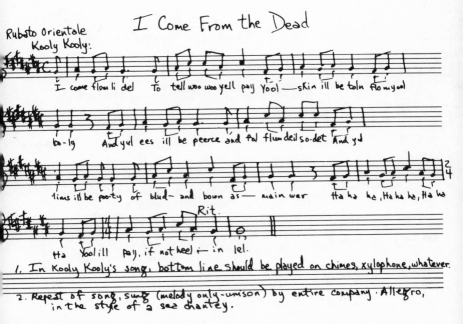

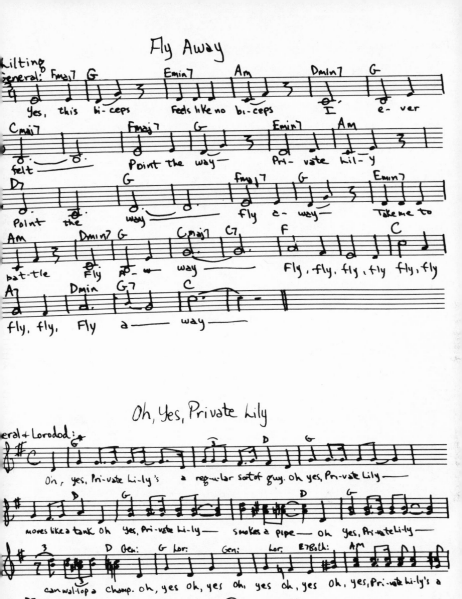

Lorodod's Song

My dar-ling   Have you no-ticed how strange-ly   the sun sub-merg-es

Be-yond the land ___ "The sun-set"   It is strange ___ The

sun is   as-u-su-al   pink, pur-ple   and sub-tle

But the land does not pro-vide the u-sual em-broi-dered out-line "Land-scape"

It is flat ___   Nor does the land con-tribute to the col-ors ___

of the scheme it's ___ u-su-al ver-dure   "Foliage"   It is grey

oh, it is gray   Have you noti-ced   how the sub-stance we stand on

the sub-stance So - il   is   brittle   And that

breath-ing   is ra-ther hard ___ "Difficult"   The air is dry.

The Boomboom Song

Vaudeville feel.

Boom, Boomboom Boomboom Boomboom Boomboom Boom ___ Boomboom Boomboom Boomboom Boomboo

Boomboom — Boom ___   Boom Boomboom Boomboom Boomboom Boomboom Boom ___

We got some mod-als for the Boom—Boom ___

DR. KHEAL

Dr. Kheal was first performed on April 15, 1968, in two simultaneous productions: one at The Village Gate, as a benefit for the Caffe Cino, and one at the New Dramatists Workshop. Both versions were directed by Remy Charlip. At the Village Gate the performer was David Tice; at the New Dramatists Workshop it was Phillip Bruns. Mr. Tice subsequently appeared in the role in a series of performances given by the Judson Poets Theatre at Judson Memorial Church, beginning August 3, 1968

There is a reading stand, a small table with a jug of water and two glasses, a blackboard, and a stand with various charts. PROFESSOR KHEAL *enters.* HE *is small, or else the furniture is large.*

DR. KHEAL   The professor picks up the chalk,

(DR. KHEAL *picks up the chalk*)

and writes.

(DR. KHEAL *writes* The Outline *on the blackboard.* HE *looks at what he wrote and decides to draw a line along the edges of the blackboard*)

He looks at the class with an air of superiority and counts to three, demanding their attention. One, two, and three. He asks his first question.

HE *mouths a question and then puts his hand to his ear as if listening to the answer.*

Wrong.

Pointing in different directions.

Wrong. Wrong. Wrong. Wrong. Then, suddenly, someone shouts his answer from the back. Others join him. They all shout at once. It becomes a loud and fast thing. The teacher speaks rapidly, trying to reply to each. Wrong, wrong, wrong, wrong, wrong, wrong, wrong. Damn it! You're wrong.

Suggesting a voice from the distance.

"Dear professor, perhaps you have the wrong answer."

HE *looks at the audience fiercely.*

My answer wrong? It couldn't be that my answer is wrong. I am the master. Let us proceed.

HE *looks among his papers, then talks to himself.*

How could my answer by wrong? . . . Hmmm . . . Did I have an answer?

HE *thinks.*

Nonsense, I don't need an answer. I am the master. . . . Let me see. . . . Let me see. . . . I'll find an answer. Hmmm . . . Hmmm . . . How is that possible? I don't even remember the question. Was there a question?

To the audience.

Was there?

To himself:

Hmm. Of course there was. There's always a question, and who knows what the answer is?

To the audience:

Raise your hand if you know the answer. . . . Ha ha. There you are! There are many of you, but the multitude is often wrong.

HE *starts to erase the blackboard.*

Is it not?

HE *looks to see if someone replies.* HE *then erases the blackboard and writes* On Poetry.

Now, poetry is for the most part a waste of time, and so is politics . . . and history . . . and philosophy. . . . Nothing concrete. Nothing like a well-made box. Which is concrete and beautiful and you can put things in it. But what can you do with poems? Tell me. And with politics, and with history, and with philosophy? —You can wrap them up, shove them up your ass, and what do you have?

HE *moves his hands as if he were doing a magic trick which ends with the middle finger up.*

. . . Nothing. . . . Ha ha ha ha ha ha.

Invaded by an immense poetic feeling.

But if you can make a box, think, have you not made a lyrical thing?

HE *thinks he hears someone speak.* HE *squints, and looks over his glasses, then ignores the possible speaker.*

Poetry, on the other hand, is just a few words put together. Just a few. Just words. There is poetry. . . . And then they say there are poets . . . poets of this sort, poets of that sort, and poets of the other sort. . . . But who, tell me, understands the poetry of space in a box? I do. . . . Abysmal and concrete at the same time. Four walls, a top, and a bottom . . . and yet a void. . . . Who understands that? I, Professor Kheal, I understand it clearly and expound it well.

Memory holds his attention.

And then, there is the smell of wood, that sober smell.

HE *takes a deep breath, then goes to the blackboard and writes* On Balance. *Then he draws the following figure:*

HE *moves away, looks at the blackboard, looks for his glasses in his pocket, puts them on, and points to the blackboard.*

Balance can save your life. Imbalance can destroy it.

Lost in his thoughts.

. . . What is balance? . . . Balance is a state of equilibrium between opposing forces. The harmonious proportions of elements in design. Balance is keeping my pants up. My groin in place.

HE *looks around with raised eyebrows for a moment.*

Any more questions?

HE *goes to the blackboard, erases, and writes* On Ambition.

Then, of course there is the question of will. Oh, will, will, will, will. Always will. Tell me, does anyone here know the evil of will?

HE *waits for an answer.*

Does anyone know the nature of will?

HE *waits for an answer.*

Does the thing happen, or does one do it? . . . Through will. Does the thing happen, or does one do it? Of course, sometimes it happens and other times one does it. I don't mean . . . just anything . . . ordinarily. . . . I mean how . . . what . . . which . . . Is *it* made. . . . Can *it* be made. . . . What? Life! Of course life. Do you know the difference between will and appetite? Can life be made? No, I don't mean birth. I mean life. The life you lead. Can I make my own life . . . Construct my own life? . . . Through will? Of course not, you fool. Of course you can. But then, a well-planned life is pitiful. Doesn't it seem richer if the firmament puts its silvery hands in it? In your life?

HE *puts his hand to his ear.*

What?

HE *listens.*

An old-fashioned thought?

HE *listens again.*

Modern thought has what? . . . Modern? . . . Mo-dern? . . .

HE *scrutinizes the speaker.*

You scum, you turd, you stale refuse. Worse than that! Plastic face!

HE *blows air through his mouth.*

That is what I think of you. . . . I'll take your will and chew on it, like a little oyster, or a clam. Chew, chew, chew, chew, chew your little will, yum yum . . . I'll chew your little entrails.

HE *darts his tongue like a satyr. Then* HE *puts his hands over his groin with a scared look.* HE *looks around the audience.*

What would you like? A show of hands? All right. Let's have a show of hands. Those in favor of the firmament leading you by the hand, raise your hands.

HE *counts.*

Those in favor of making your own life raise your hands.

HE *counts.*

All I can do is peepee before you.

HE *raises his leg like a dog and then shakes it.*

And the rest, those who did not raise your hands—what do you think? Is there another alternative? Either you do it, or else it does itself. Life, that is. What other way is there? None.

HE *looks suspiciously at a few.*

None. There is no other way. All right.

HE *erases the blackboard and writes* On Energy. HE *goes to the chart stand.*

Here is the next question.

HE *unrolls a chart that reads: "How does one do a million little things?"*

How does one do a million little things? . . . What is the answer? How does one do a million little things?

HE *waits a moment for the answer.*

One at a time.

HE *is pleased with the incisiveness of his answer.*

Now.

HE *unrolls the next chart. It reads: "How does one do a million big things?"*

How does one do a million big things? . . . Hmmm . . . Does anyone know the answer?

HE *waits a moment.*

One at a time. Ha ha ha ha ha . . . What a surprise. . . . Surprised, everyone? Now, the last of the three.

HE *unrolls the next chart. It reads: "How does one do one big thing?"*

How does one do one big thing? . . . Ha ha ha ha ha ha ha.
Extraordinary question, isn't it? I'll answer it.

HE *goes to the blackboard and makes this drawing:*

Pointing to where the arrow indicates:

Start here.

HE *fills in the space indicated as follows:*

HE *darts his tongue like a satyr.*

Would you have guessed? Never.

HE *erases the blackboard and writes* On Speech.

Now . . . words change the nature of things. A thing not named and the same thing named are two different things. Ha ha ha ha . . . The ways of the Devil . . . that son of a gun. . . . Someone once said, "In the beginning was the word." Guess who? The Devil . . . clever bastard. He'd say anything. In the beginning was not the word. He names things to make them other than what we know them to be. Then he renames them. So the name he first gave them becomes separate from the thing, and we are left without the word or the thing, the new word having none of the spirit of the first. Think of the word "sin." The Devil first named sin to make the thing we did other than what we knew it to be. Then, once we understood what sin was and learned to sin and repent, and sin and repent again, and we had a clear understanding of what sin was, the Devil, in order to deprive us of this knowledge, decided to declare the word void. Today you say the word "sin," and little frigid minds (the Devil's assistants) snub you. So you recoil and quickly say something accepted by these frigid little minds. "Guilt." And their expression of smug condescension changes to one of smug comprehension. In their minds, the word "sin" has been dispossessed of its meaning and "guilt" has been sanctioned by reason. Today who dares to speak of freedom . . . goodness . . . happiness? . . . Happiness . . . Who dares to say the word without some kind of *(Mocking their manner)* "Intellectual hesitation." *(Still mockingly)* "Happiness . . . happiness. . . . What do you mean by happiness?" *(Back to himself)* And I show them my teeth.

HE *opens his mouth wide, then puts his fingers in his mouth.*

And I say to them, here is happiness. My teeth are good. That makes me happy.

Forcing his hand in the mouth of an imaginary person.

And I put my whole hand in their mouths and I call them every name in the book. Violent! I am. I get angry. But it doesn't matter. I am always right. You see, we who speak must not let words turn upside down on us and turn us into fools.

HE *goes to the blackboard, erases, and writes* On Truth.

Most people believe that truth is the order in which they live. Others, the bright ones, believe that there is no truth at all but only an arrangement. Both are mistaken. Ha ha ha ha ha ha. Now, truth is not at all the way we understand things to be. Why? The moment you name it, it is gone. A chair. You name it: "Chair," and there it is, still a chair. A dog. You name it: "Dog," and it comes. But truth . . . you name it and it vanishes. What is truth then? Anyone know?

HE *stands like a bullfighter and makes three rapid passes.*

There is truth. Three quick passes. Name it here, here, and here. Surround it, and you'll have it. Never touch it. It will vanish. That is truth . . . elusive.

HE *goes to the blackboard and erases. Then* HE *writes* Anecdote.

On my way here this evening someone said to me . . . "Dr. Kheal, is being poor a sign of stinginess?"

HE *opens his mouth as if to laugh, but makes no sound.*

I said, no, it isn't. *(Pause)* But of course it is. *(Pause)* Ha ha ha ha.

HE *erases the blackboard and writes* On Beauty and Love,

The morning was fine. I cleaned the bathroom, then the kitchen. What else is there but cleanliness?

HE *looks over his glasses expecting objections.*

And then, I lay down to rest with my head on a high pillow. "Gee, look at my belly going up and down. I must be alive." Well . . . in that case . . . I go to my dresser, I look in the mirror. "Gee, look how pleasant my face is in the mirror, I must be beautiful." Ha ha ha. Well, we each have our way. I know that we can only do what is possible. I know that. We can only do what is possible for us to do. But still it is good to know what the impossible is.

There is a pause. HE *is looking at the impossible.*

Beauty is . . . the impossible. . . . Beauty . . . beauty . . . Crissanda, thou art the impossible. . . . Beauty . . . what art thou that drives me out of my mind? Beauty . . . Shall I tell you?

HE *sees Crissanda in front of him.*

She speaks in riddles, like the gods. "ksjdnhyidfgesles." She says:

HE *chants the following.*

"I am the supreme lover. I bring you bliss. . . . Listen to me. . . . Listen. . . . I know . . ."

Back to his own voice.

The fool, she knows nothing. I just love the way she talks. She chants in riddles, like the gods. "ksjdudyehrs." She says:

Chanting again.

"Don't move your hands when you talk. It tickles me. From the distance, the movements of your hands tickle me."

Back to himself.

And I laugh. . . . And I move my hands. Ha ha ha ha.

HE *pauses.* HE *looks at Crissanda.*

And she looked at me surprised, and her little eye wandered and was lost.

HE *watches her vanish.*

"Where are you?" I said, "my little one . . . Crissanda . . . don't go . . . I didn't mean to laugh." And she appeared in the distance . . . just for a moment . . . just to say: "Crazy people are fools.

Making his voice faint.

You fool . . . you fool . . . you fool. . . ."

His eyes are open very wide. They are filled with tears.

And she left. "Crissanda, Crissanda," I called after her. . . . She was gone. . . . What happened? What happened . . . I know what happened and yet I cannot say. I do not know the words to speak of beauty and of love. I, who know everything. . . . Some things are impossible. . . .

HE *goes to the blackboard.*

Love, as we know it, increases daily. Let us say the average level of love is 100 degrees. We add a daily increase of 10. We subtract 7 for daily wear and tear and we have a daily increase of 3 which is cumulative. In 10 days we have an increase of 30 which has raised the level to 130. We have a big fight which reduces the level by 50, leaving love at a low level of 80. However, the daily increase of 10 minus daily wear and tear of 7 continues . . . producing a true increase of 3 which is cumulative. After 7 days we have an increase of 3 times 7 which is 21. Added to the low level of 80 we have 101. Back to normal.

HE *has written the following:*

100	10	7
+10	×3	×3
110	30	21
−7	+100	+80
103	130	101
	−50	
	80	

Here is the arithmetic of love. Ha! You think that is contradictory? Love and mathematics? Don't you know that you can take a yes and a no and push them together, squeeze them together, compress them so they are one? That in fact that is what reality is? Opposites, contradictions compressed so that you don't know where one stops and the other begins? . . . Let us proceed.

HE *erases, and writes* On Hope.

And here, is a picture of hope.

HE *draws the following picture as* HE *describes it.*

Man stands in his life, "Grotto." Always with a sense of being enclosed. He thinks of freedom, open space, air, sun. The only way out is always narrow, always arduous and frightening to cross. He dares. He fills his lungs with air. He swims. He is courageous. He reaches the point where, if he goes any further, he won't be able to return. "Point of no return." If he continues he might find the exit, if there is an exit . . . if the exit is within reach of his endurance. That is the point. Does he continue? Does he return? There, is the picture of hope.

HE *erases and writes* On Cooking.

Have you ever cooked brussel sprouts? The miniature cabbage? Toy vegetable? Have you ever seen how beautiful they are?

HE *erases and writes* Summing Up.

And now, to conclude, I'll sing you a song.

The other day,
Looking at a weird-looking spider,
With legs ten times longer than its body,
Who moved in the most senseless and
Insane manner,
I said, "Spider, you are spastic and I am
A superior beast."

There! That is what it is all about.
Man is the rational animal.

HE *exits.*

MOLLY'S DREAM

To Aileen Passloff

Molly's Dream was first performed by the Boston
University Writers Conference in Tanglewood,
Massachusetts, on July 23, 1968. This workshop staging was
directed by Edward Setrakian, with music by Cosmos
Savage, costumes by Miss Fornés, lighting by Thomas
Munn, and the following cast:

Molly   *Diane Kagin*
The Young Man   *Peter Masterson*
Mack   *Bill Gerber*
John   *Leonard Hicks*
Alberta   *Crystal Field*
The Hanging Women   *Lisa Billock, Diane Birken, Tina
    Takayanagi, Julia Ann Goldsmith, Myla Zinn, Carolyn
    Clowes*

A revised version was subsequently performed at the New
Dramatists Workshop in New York on December 5, 1968.
This workshop production was directed and designed by the
author, with musical accompaniment by David Tice,
lighting by Therese King, and the following cast:

Molly   *Julie Bovasso*
The Young Man   *Ray Barry*
Mack   *Jim Cashman*
John   *Leonard Hicks*
Alberta   *Crystal Field*
The Hanging Women   *Carol Gelfand (soloist), Kay Carney, Penny Dupont, Margaret Impert, Alice Tweedy*

Photograph:
Molly and Mack,
New Dramatists
production

CHARACTERS

MOLLY: Late twenties. A waitress.

THE YOUNG MAN: Late twenties. A laborer.

JIM: He is played by the same actor as the YOUNG MAN but he appears endowed with sublime sex appeal.

THE HANGING WOMEN: A chorus of five.

MACK: A bartender in his forties.

JOHN: A lean middle-aged cowboy.

ALBERTA: A 27-year-old, who refuses to grow.

Part I:
Molly and the Hanging Women

An old-fashioned saloon typical of warm climates. There are several swinging doors on both sides. Both sides of the saloon lead to streets. Another swinging door on the back wall leads to the kitchen. The counter is alongside the back wall. A trap door on the floor behind the counter leads to the basement.
There are fans hanging from the ceiling, potted plants, spittoons, tables, and chairs. There is a wall mirror, and a cage with a bird. On the counter there is a gun, and the two porcelain figures— one in the shape of a woman; the other, Cupid. A top hat hangs from a hat rack.
The play of lights indicated in the script denotes an important moment in the life of one or another character.
MOLLY is alone in the tavern. SHE wears a black satin uniform. SHE prepares herself a cup of coffee, takes off her shoes, sits down and begins to read to herself from a magazine.

MOLLY   (SHE *mumbles some of the following words and begins to act them out*) Rosie was a darned good waitress. She wasn't the kind that would spill any whiskey on the counter. But when Sam started walking toward her, her hand started shaking, and the whiskey spilled. Sam, her beloved Sam, whom she was even thinking of marrying, had shot at the Sheriff. What a thing to do. This broke her heart and made her nervous. That's why she spilled the drink. Sam, who seemed like such a nice guy, had shot at the Sheriff and now he had the nerve to come into the tavern as if nothing had happened, or at least he had the nerve to come into the tavern. He pulled a chair from one of the tables, turned it toward him and straddled it. He looked at her for a while without saying anything. Then he said, "Are you angry because I shot at the Sheriff?" *(MOLLY puts the magazine down and takes a puff from her cigarette. SHE speaks the following dialogue out loud, acting out both characters in the story)* "Are you angry because I shot at the Sheriff?" *(Sarcastically)* "Naw, I was getting tired of his face. I wouldn't mind seeing someone else wear that star. What would you like?"

One of the swinging doors opens slightly. The YOUNG MAN *puts his head in.* MOLLY *does not notice him.*

"Let me have a steak . . . rare. . . . And don't bother putting arsenic in the gravy." *(MOLLY writes in her check pad)* "Rare, no arsenic." Oh, boy.

MOLLY *notices the* YOUNG MAN. SHE *is flustered.* THEY *look at one another for a moment.* HE *smiles and walks away.* MOLLY *begins to feel sleepy.* SHE *yawns.* SHE *leans her head on the table and falls asleep. A dreamlike atmosphere is suggested by means of lights, smoke, or the lifting of the walls. A swinging door opens.* JIM *puts his head in.* HE *looks exactly like the* YOUNG MAN *and is played by the same actor.*

JIM   *(Suspiciously)* Is there a waiter here?

MOLLY   *(Raising her head)* Yes.

JIM enters. HE is dressed in glittering lace. HE looks like a prince in a fairy tale. FIVE WOMEN surround him as if THEY were a floating part of him. These are the HANGING WOMEN. When HE is still, THEY hang on to him gently. HE sits at a table. MOLLY stretches and walks to him. SHE waits for his order.

JIM   Isn't there a waiter here?

MOLLY   Yes, me.

JIM   I mean a man waiter.

MOLLY   No, there's just me.

JIM looks at MOLLY for a moment. Then HE stands and walks to the door.

JIM   I don't need one more woman.

As JIM exits, the doors swing. MACK enters with a box of soda bottles, goes behind the counter and disappears behind it. JIM puts his head through the doors again.

Didn't I just see a man behind the bar?

MOLLY   Yes.

JIM   Where did he go?

MOLLY   He's in the basement.

JIM   Is he coming back?

MOLLY   Mack!

MACK   What?

MOLLY   Are you coming back?

MACK   Yes.

MOLLY   Yes, he is coming back.

JIM *starts walking toward the same table where* HE *sat before.*

JIM   I thought you said there was no waiter.

MOLLY   He's not a waiter.

JIM   *(Stopping)* What is he?

MOLLY   Bartender.

JIM *walks to the bar. A few moments pass.* MOLLY *looks at him with curiosity.* HE *tries to avoid her glance.* MACK *appears behind the bar.*

JIM   A double rye, please.

MACK *pours a drink.* JIM *takes the drink to a table.*

MACK   Boy, that's a man for you. . . . Look at that.

MACK *exits.* MOLLY *sits at* JIM*'s table and looks at the* HANGING WOMEN.

MOLLY   Who are they?

JIM *drinks his rye in one gulp.*

JIM   Who?

MOLLY *points to the* HANGING WOMEN.

Friends.

MOLLY   What's the matter with them?

JIM   Nothing is the matter with them.

MOLLY   Why are they hovering around you like that?

JIM   They like me.

>   MOLLY *looks at the* HANGING WOMEN.

MOLLY   Doesn't it bother you to have them . . .

>   SHE *gestures.* JIM *shakes his head.*

JIM   A little.

MOLLY   Why don't you tell them to scoot?

JIM   I have.

MOLLY   And?

JIM   They won't go.

MOLLY   *(Waving her hands as if to scare away chickens)* Shhh . . .
Shhh . . .

>   *The* HANGING WOMEN *flutter.*

JIM   Don't do that. . . . You'll hurt their feelings.

>   JIM *looks for* MACK. *While his head is turned* MOLLY *waves her arms with sweeping movements.*

MOLLY   Shh . . . Shhh . . .

The HANGING WOMEN *scatter all over the room.* THEY *are breathless and in a state of anxiety. The lights flash on and remain strong through the following scene.*

They're off.

JIM *is also breathless and in a state of anxiety.*

What's the matter?

JIM *gasps for air.*

I thought you wanted them off.

HANGING WOMEN   *(Sing)*

Do not collapse just now, world.
Do not collapse just now.
Wait a bit. Wait a bit.
Perhaps I can find my way back.

MOLLY   I thought you wanted them off.

The HANGING WOMEN *start moving toward* JIM.

JIM

Oh . . . oh . . . oh . . . oh . . .
The flower of love grew on me,
And she pulled,
She pulled it off.

The HANGING WOMEN *surround him again.* MOLLY *pats them.*

MOLLY   It's all right now.

JIM

>   It grew from my side.
>   It grew from my legs.
>   It grew from my arms.
>   The most beautiful thing grew off me.
>   The flower of love.
>   And she pulled it off.

HANGING WOMEN   *(Sing)*

>   Oh . . . oh . . . oh . . .

MOLLY   It's all right . . . you're back.

HANGING WOMEN

>   It's just that I hear
>   A little bit of love
>   Going down the drain.
>   Glop, glop, glop,
>   Going down the drain.

JIM

>   She put them back.
>   But she had pulled them off.
>   She had pulled them off.
>   Oh, God, she pulled them off.

MOLLY   Gee whiz.

>   *The lights go back to normal.* JIM *looks for* MACK.

>   What do you want?

JIM   I thought I'd ask him for a drink. But that's all right.

MOLLY   *(Standing)* Double?

JIM   Don't bother.

MOLLY   It's no bother. That's what I'm here for.

JIM   I changed my mind. I don't want a drink.

   MOLLY *sits.*

MOLLY   Are you broke?

JIM   No.

MOLLY   It's on the house.

JIM   Why?

   MOLLY *stares at* JIM *and speaks distractedly.* HE *recognizes the look and becomes cautious.*

MOLLY   Oh, I don't know. I just thought I'd buy you a drink.

JIM   Why?

MOLLY   Why? . . . That's how I felt. . . . I felt like buying you a drink. (SHE *walks toward* JIM)

JIM   Oh, God . . . Well, don't buy me a drink. You go on out in there.

MOLLY   Where?

JIM   In the kitchen. Go in the kitchen and do what you have to do. Wash some glasses.

MOLLY   I don't wash the glasses. Mack does that.

JIM   Well . . . read your magazine. . . . Don't come so close.

MOLLY   . . . Why not? *(SHE is very close to him)*

JIM   Oh, God.

>   MOLLY *throws her arms around* JIM *'s neck and lets herself hang. The lights flash on and off.*

Listen . . . lady . . . excuse me a moment. Hey, miss . . .

MOLLY   *(Still hanging)* What?

JIM   Do I owe you anything?

MOLLY   I don't know.

JIM   Think about it for a moment.

MOLLY   I can't think now.

JIM   Look, I don't owe you anything. You have to let go.

>   MOLLY *returns to her chair.*

MOLLY   Well, what do you expect. I was curious.

JIM   That's all right. Just don't do it again.

>   MACK *enters.*

MACK   . . . That's a man for you.

JIM   Double rye, please.

MACK *pours the drink and exits.* JIM *starts to stand.*

MOLLY   I'll get it.

JIM   No, it's all right. I'll get it.

MOLLY   *(Going to the bar)* I'll get it. It's my job.

JIM   No, it's all right. I'd like to get my own drink if you don't mind.

MOLLY   That's all right. I'm the waitress. *(SHE reaches for the drink)*

JIM   It's my drink. I get my own drink if I want to.

MOLLY   You can't get your own drink. I get paid to get the drinks.

JIM   It's my drink. I'm paying for it and I don't want any favors.

MOLLY   It's no favor. It's my job.

> JIM *grabs her.* THEY *struggle for a moment.* SHE *manages to put the drink on the table.*

Just leave me a tip.

JIM   You don't need a tip.

MOLLY   What do I need?

JIM   Love.

> MOLLY *hangs again.* MACK *enters.*

MACK   You didn't have to bother. Molly would have brought it to you. Where's Molly? *(Discovering her)* Molly . . .

> MOLLY *doesn't answer.*

Molly, what are you doing?

MOLLY   I'll be up in a minute.

MACK   What do you mean you'll be up in a minute? Molly . . . what in the world are you doing?

JIM   She'll never let go.

MACK   How do you do it?

JIM   It's a burden.

MACK   I wish I had that burden.

JIM   They weigh a lot.

MACK   Leave them home. You don't know how to handle women.

JIM   I can't leave them home. It would hurt their feelings.

MACK   Hurt their feelings? What's the matter with you. Are you a sissy?

JIM   I don't want to hurt their feelings.

MACK   Hey, Molly, forget it, kid. This guy's a sissy.

SHE *ignores him.*

Hey, Molly, what's the matter with you? He's a sissy.

MOLLY   Shut up, Mack.

JIM   Bunch of creeps.

MACK   That's the trouble with women. Here's me, a real man. You name it, I have it. There's that creep . . . a sissy. . . . Do they go for me? No. They go for him . . . a sissy. *(MACK starts moving furniture as if to prepare for cleaning the floor)* A burden he says . . . women a burden . . . wish I had that burden. I could take on a hundred. One right after the other. No problem. A hundred. Bang, bang, bang. Just like that. *(Sings)*

Bang bang bang bang
Bang
Bang bang bang bang
Bang
Bang
Bang
Bang

The HANGING WOMEN *surround* MACK.

MACK AND THE HANGING WOMEN

Bang bang bang bang
Bang bang bang bang
Bang bang bang bang
Bang bang bang bang
Bang bang bang bang
Bang
Bang bang bang bang
Bang
Bang
Bang

Bang bang bang bang
Bang bang bang bang
Bang bang bang bang
Bang bang bang bang
Bang bang bang bang
Bang
Bang bang bang bang
Bang
Bang
Bang

Bang bang bang bang
Bang bang bang bang
Bang bang bang bang
Bang bang bang bang
Bang bang bang bang
Bang
Bang bang bang bang
Bang
Bang
Bang

MACK   *(Spoken)* But do they go for me? . . . No.

The HANGING WOMEN *put their hands on* MACK. HE *collapses.*

HANGING WOMEN   Creep!

The HANGING WOMEN *go back to* JIM. MACK *stands.* HE *turns to the* HANGING WOMEN *the way a wrestler waits for an attack.*

MACK   Try again. . . . Come on. . . . Come on. . . . Try again. I can take the lot of you. You yellow-bellied broads.

HANGING WOMEN   Creep!

MACK   Aw, bunch of dumb broads.

JOHN *enters.* HE *wears black dungarees, a black shirt, a cowboy hat, and holsters with guns from his ankles to his armpits.*

Hey, Molly, a customer.

MOLLY *does not respond.*

Hey, Molly.

MOLLY   What?

MACK Customer.

MOLLY Wait a moment.

JIM Molly . . .

MOLLY What?

JIM Are you going to stay? *(Pause)* Molly, are you going to stay? *(Pause)* I like you, Molly, but I just can't take on any more. (HE *waits a moment)* Listen, you have to let go.

MOLLY I don't want to.

JIM Well, you have to.

MOLLY *lets go.*

Are your feelings hurt?

MOLLY *(Hurt)* No.

JIM Molly, I can't take on any more. I just can't. I can hardly walk as it is. I can't play baseball. Do you understand what it is not to be able to play baseball? I just can't take on any more. And besides, I don't owe you anything.

MOLLY Well, I liked it.

JIM All right then, hang on. What's one more?

MOLLY Not unless the others leave.

JIM I can't tell them to leave.

MOLLY   Why not?

JIM   I'm indebted to them.

MOLLY   Why?

JIM   Because . . . they like me.

MOLLY   That's nothing.

JIM   I'm indebted to them.

MOLLY   I can do more than that for a man.

JIM   I know, you're different.

MOLLY   So?

JIM   Molly, I can't.

MOLLY   You said I was different.

JIM   I'm indebted to them.

> MOLLY *dries a tear, starts to walk away. Then turns to the* HANGING WOMEN *and starts waving her arms.*

MOLLY   Shhh . . . Shhh . . .

JIM   Mollyyy! Don't!

MOLLY   Creep!

> *The lights flash on and remain strong through the following scene.* MOLLY *takes off her apron.* SHE *gradually develops a German accent.* SHE *begins to behave in a manner resembling Marlene Dietrich.*

MACK   Molly . . . Customer.

MOLLY   *(To* JOHN*)* What do you want?

JOHN *thinks a moment and begins to make a gesture.*

Whisky, double, very straight, hold the chaser, make it fast. He's dry.

JOHN   Make it a Bloody Mary.

MACK   *(While preparing the drink)* What was it like?

MOLLY   I can't explain it.

MACK   Try.

MOLLY   It felt right. That's all.

MACK   Come on.

MOLLY   You have to live it. You can't explain it.

MACK   *(Pouring whiskey for* MOLLY*)* It's for you.

MOLLY   *(*SHE *drinks it)* Thanks.

MACK   Now, tell me.

MOLLY   What.

MACK   What was it like?

MOLLY   It felt right.

MACK   That doesn't mean anything.

MOLLY   It felt right to be near him.

MACK   That's nothing.

MOLLY   It's everything, you dumb creep. You'd never understand.

MACK   Well, explain it to me.

MOLLY   I can't explain it. Try it yourself.

MACK   What do you think I am?

MOLLY   Forget it then.

MACK   Are you going back?

MOLLY   Never again. *(SHE walks to JOHN's table with his drink)*

MACK   Ha ha.

MOLLY   What does that mean? Ha ha.

MACK   He's not so good.

MOLLY   He's good all right. I'm just not going back.

MOLLY *drinks JOHN's drink.* SHE *then goes to the bar and sits on it.*

MACK   What do you mean by drinking the customer's drink?

MOLLY *shrugs her shoulders.*

Who do you think you are.

MACK *pours another drink for JOHN.* MOLLY *lights a cigarette.* Here, bring it to him.

MOLLY *does not respond.*

Hey, Molly! . . . Kid! . . . Bring the customer his drink.

MOLLY *puffs some smoke.*

MOLLY   Molly kid was. Are you blind, you creep? Can't you see what life has done to me? Molly kid was. I have just changed my name.

The music starts.

No. I'm not breaking into song. The moment is too sad. I'm not going back. Good as he is, my feelings are hurt.

JIM   Molly, come back.

MOLLY   Molly was. I have just changed my name

The music plays louder as if to invite her to sing.

No. Little Molly would have sung, do re mi fa sol la ti, not me.

JIM   Molly, come back.

MOLLY   Not me. My feelings are hurt. Broken to pieces.

SHE *pushes the figurine in the shape of a woman off the counter. It crashes on the floor.* MACK *picks up the pieces.*

JIM   Come back, Molly.

MACK *starts putting the pieces together.*

MOLLY   Don't bother to put the pieces together, Mack. It will never be the same. Throw it away.

MACK *throws the pieces in a garbage can. The sound pains*
MOLLY.

Good-bye, Molly . . . poor kid . . . she's gone. *(Taking the figure
of Cupid)* Perhaps you're too young to know how it hurts to love.
. . . It hurts.

MOLLY *and* JIM *stare at each other for a while.* SHE *looks away
from him, showing her profile.* SHE *puts her foot up on the bar,
puts a top hat on and her elbow on her knee.*

It seems I did my song after all. *(*SHE *rests her head on her hand)*

MACK   OK, Molly, get off the bar.

MOLLY   Shut up, Mack.

JIM   Molly.

MACK   Get your feet off the bar. I won't have anybody putting their
feet on the bar.

JIM   Leave her alone.

MACK   Who do you think you are? You come in here and look at
the way she's acting. She's acting like a nut. She never acted like
that before.

JIM   I know, I just broke her heart.

MACK   Molly.

MOLLY   Huh.

MACK   Look at her. *(To* MOLLY*)* What's the matter with you?

MOLLY   Nothing is the matter with me. What are you talking
about?

MACK   You're acting like a nut.

MOLLY   I'm not acting like a nut.

MACK   You better do something about her. I won't have anybody sitting at the bar.

JIM   I will. . . . *(To* MOLLY*)* Molly.

MOLLY   What?

JIM   You used to be a nice kid.

MOLLY   No more. Those are bygone days.

MACK   Well, somebody bring the customer his drink, or I'm not responsible for my acts.

   MOLLY *takes a puff of her cigarette.* JIM *takes the drink to* JOHN *as* JOHN *goes to the bar.*

What do you want?

JOHN   I thought I'd get the drink myself.

MACK   It's on the table.

   JOHN *goes to his table.*

I'm glad you brought him the drink, otherwise I couldn't have answered for my acts.

JIM   I didn't do it for you. I did it for her.

JOHN   Thanks, I was beginning to get thirsty.

JIM   That's all right. I did it for her. *(Going to* MOLLY*)* Molly . . .

MOLLY   Hm.

JIM   Molly, I didn't mean to hurt you.

MOLLY   You can't hurt me. I have no heart.

JIM   You do, Molly, you have a heart.

MOLLY   I don't have a heart.

JIM   Molly, If I told you that I loved you, would you get off the bar?

MOLLY   No.

MACK   He's a sissy.

JIM   I am responsible . . . *(*HE *sings)*

    I accept,
    I accept,
    I accept
    The responsibility of my enormous sex appeal.
    If a woman says she loves me,
    I cannot tell her to go.

    I breathe hot,
    I breathe hot,
    I breathe hot,
    And I breathe hot.
    No woman has ever resisted me, and I accept,
    The responsibility.

    J'accepte,
    J'accepte,
    J'accepte,
    La responsabilité de mon énorme sex-appeal.

I cannot turn them away.
J'accepte
Les conséquences désastreuses de mon énorme sex-appeal.

I never said to a woman,
I love you.
But I accept,
I accept
The responsibility.

HANGING WOMEN   *(Sing)*

To a woman you will say,
I love you.
She will not understand.
You will say,
I love you.
You will say,
I love you, twice.
Twice you'll say it.
I love you. I love you.
And then she'll understand.
Je t'aime. Je t'aime.

JIM *turns to* MOLLY. *His face is close to hers.*

JIM   *Je t'aime.*

MOLLY *turns her head to look at* JIM *and does not reply.*

I love you.

MOLLY *blows smoke in his face and smiles.* JIM *coughs.* HE *is downcast. The* HANGING WOMEN *move away from him.* JIM *walks to center stage and stands on his head with one leg bent and crossed, in a position resembling the Hanged Man of the Tarot.*

HANGING WOMEN

To a woman he said,
I love you.
She did not understand.
He said,
I love you.
But she did not understand.
He said,
I love you, twice.
Twice he said it.
Je t'aime. I love you.
And then she understood.
But not a word came out of her mouth.
Only smoke.
And he lost his charm.
All his charm was lost.

(Spoken) Now, you're as common as Mack.

MACK   And who said I'm common, you dumb broads. I can take on
the whole lot of you, you yellow-bellied broads. Bang, bang,
bang, just like that.

JIM *stands on his feet and sits at a table. The lights are dimmed
except for a spot on* JIM.

INTERLUDE

JIM   *(Sings)*

And what has my noble face offered the world?
A smile.
Yes, it has done that.
A gentle look? Yes, my noble face has done that.

And what else have I offered the world?
A few kind words, perhaps.
And some elusive words.

And what have my loving eyes given the world?
A remorseful stare.
And who am I?
Am I the wrongdoer or the wronged?

I never raised my hand to hurt a man.
And yet, I ask: Who am I,
The wrongdoer or the wronged?

My life is filled with doubt, fear,
And desire distrust.
And yet I do not know:
Am I the wrongdoer or the wronged?

And what have my hands done?
They have reached out with love.
And the loved one has turned to me and said:
Who are you?. . . Who are you?

I'm the wrongdoer.
That's who I am.

The lights come up.

Part II:
Dracula the Misunderstood
There is no time lapse between Part One and Part Two.

JOHN   *(To* JIM*)* Blackjack, sir?

JIM   What . . .

JOHN   Blackjack?

JIM *looks* JOHN *over and nods.* JOHN *shuffles the cards expecting* JIM *to come to his table.* JIM *pushes a chair away from his table with his foot inviting* JOHN *to come to his.* JOHN *shuffles the cards again, cuts them twice and looks at* JIM. JIM *challenges* JOHN *by remaining where* HE *is.* JOHN *picks up the cards and holds them thinking what to do. Then,* HE *puts two cards on the table face down and sneaks a look at* JIM *who remains seated.* HE *looks at his card, then at* JIM*'s and smiles feebly.*

You win.

HE *goes to* JIM. *Through the following scene* JOHN *puts a dollar on the table,* JIM *puts a dollar on the table.* JIM *deals two cards each.* ONE *of the* HANGING WOMEN *joins the* PLAYERS *at their table and watches the game.*

MOLLY   Give me a drink, Joe.

MACK   My name is not Joe.

MOLLY   Give me a drink.

MACK   What do you want?

MOLLY   Give me an absinthe.

MACK   You give me a pain. Did you guys hear that?

JOHN   What?

MACK   She wants an absinthe.

MOLLY   That's what we drink in the islands.

MACK   What islands?

MOLLY *thinks a while.*

JIM   Make it two.

JOHN   Make it three.

MACK   *(Referring to* MOLLY*)* Creep.

JOHN   Hit me.

(JIM *gives* JOHN *a card.)*

Hit me again.

(JIM *gives* JOHN *a card.)*

Hit me again.

(JIM *gives* JOHN *a card.)*

Hit me again.

(JIM *gives* JOHN *a card.)*

Hit me again.

JIM   How many cards have you got? You must be over.

JOHN   No, I'm not. Hit me again.

JIM *gives* JOHN *a card suspiciously.*

Hit me again.

THEY *Indian-wrestle through the following scene.* MACK *puts three glasses on the counter.*

MOLLY   Mack, set them up, Joe.

MACK   The name is Mack.

MOLLY   Set them up.

> MOLLY *walks to the* PLAYERS, *and puts one foot up on the fourth chair.* SHE *puts a flower behind* JOHN'*s ear and kisses the* HANGING WOMAN.
>
> *Then,* SHE *considers a moment, takes the flower and puts it behind her own ear. Then* SHE *moves as if to kiss* JOHN, *changes her mind, puts the flower behind the* HANGING WOMAN'*s ear. Then* SHE *takes the flower and holds it over her lips as* SHE *tries to remember such a scene from the film* Morocco. SHE *then eats the flower.* SHE *starts walking toward the counter humming "One for My Baby."* SHE *is not satisfied with the song. Then starts humming "My Man."* SHE *is happier with that tune.*

> He isn't true.
> He beats me too.
> What can I do?

> He isn't true.
> He beats me too.
> What can I do?

> I don't really let anyone beat me.

MACK   So why do you keep saying it?

MOLLY   I like saying it.

MACK   *I like saying it. I like saying it.*

MOLLY   *(Sings)*

> He isn't true.
> He beats me too.
> What can I do?

MACK   Phony! You want a sock in the jaw? Why don't you guys do something about this dame? She gives me a pain.

MOLLY *takes a gun from the counter and puts a bullet through* JOHN*'s hand, which ends the Indian wrestling.*

JIM   Thanks. *(To* JOHN*)* Stay?

JOHN   Hit me again.

JIM *gives* JOHN *a suspicious and threatening look.* JOHN *looks at the cards.*

I'm good.

JIM   *(Dealing himself a card)* I'm busted.

JOHN   I win. *(*JOHN *puts the two dollars on his side of the table)*

JIM   Show me.

JOHN *shuffles all cards and puts seven on the table.* JIM *puts the two dollars on his side of the table.* THEY *Indian-wrestle.* MOLLY *takes the gun and puts a bullet through* JIM*'s hand.*

JOHN   Thanks. *(*JOHN *takes the two dollars, and puts one back on the table.* HE *takes the cards)* I'm dealer.

JIM   Forget it.

JOHN   What do you mean, forget it?

JIM   I'm not playing. *(To* MACK*)* How about that drink?

MACK *signals* MOLLY *to take the drinks to the table.* MOLLY *throws the glasses over her shoulder, one at a time.* JIM *catches them and throws them back.* THEY *juggle the glasses for a while.* JIM *fails to catch them.* THEY *fall to his feet.*

You make me feel frustrated.

MOLLY   How's that?

JIM   First you hang on and you like it, and then you ignore me.

MOLLY   Who, me?

JIM   Yes, you.

> ALBERTA *enters.* SHE *wears a Shirley Temple wig and a child's dress.*

MACK   *(Signaling* MOLLY *to get* ALBERTA *out)* Hey, Molly.

MOLLY   My name is not Molly.

JIM   What is your name?

MOLLY   I'm not telling anyone.

JIM   You could tell me.

MOLLY   I'm not telling.

JIM   What's the good of having a name if you don't tell anyone?

MOLLY   It's good. That way no one can call me.

JIM   I might want to write you a note.

MOLLY   I wouldn't read it anyway. *(*SHE *goes to* JOHN*)* Hey, handsome.

JIM   Don't talk to him. He's a fake.

MOLLY   What do you mean?

JIM   He never got laid in his life.

JOHN *threatens* JIM. *The lights flash on and off.*

ALBERTA   He's cute.

MACK   *(To* ALBERTA*)* I told you, no children allowed.

ALBERTA *taps to a chair and sits.* MACK *taps her shoulder.*

Out.

SHE *ignores him.* MACK *takes her by the collar out the door.*

Yeah. You wouldn't believe it, would you? Smart aleck. Can't
bear her. She dances all the time.

JOHN   She's an interesting-looking dame.

MOLLY   If you're not interested in me I was not interested in you
first.

JIM   Can't even think straight.

MOLLY   I can think straight. I just don't want to.

JOHN   Let me have another drink. Don't give me any more of that
licorice stuff. Give me a man's drink.

MACK   Like what?

MOLLY   Absinthe is a man's drink. If you drink a lot of it you go
blind.

JOHN   Give me an absinthe. *(*HE *gives* JIM *an assertive look, then
drinks the absinthe in one gulp)* Yes, that child is certainly an
interesting-looking dame. *(*HE *gives* JIM *another assertive look
and speaks to* MACK*)* Let me have another one of those. I don't
care if I do go blind.

MACK *pours.*

JIM   *(To himself)* He never got laid in his life.

JOHN   I'll have another.

MACK   You didn't drink that one yet.

    HE *drinks it, belches several times and checks his vision.*

JOHN   *(To MACK, attempting to be casual.)* Why do you think he said
I never got laid?

MACK   Don't pay any attention to him. He's a creep.

JOHN   Ask him.

MACK   Hey, why did you say . . .

JIM   *(Interrupting)* All he's got is guns.

MACK   He's got more than guns. I bet you he's got more than guns.

JIM   *(Putting a dollar on the table)* I bet all he's got is guns.

MACK   *(Putting a dollar on the table)* I bet he's got more.

    JOHN *does the "One Narrow Idea" dance. The dance consists of
making the guns swing back and forth. The lights go to full
intensity and remain so through the dance.*

JOHN   *(Sings)*

One very long,
Very narrow
Idea.

One very long
And narrow
Idea.

A narrow idea.
An old idea.
A withered idea
Without reward.
A withering idea.
An old, old idea.

MACK   *(Taking the two dollars)* Yup, he's got more than guns.

JIM   *(Taking the two dollars from* MACK*)* No, he doesn't.

THEY *Indian wrestle.* JOHN *helps* MACK *push* JIM*'s arm down.*

MACK   *(Taking the two dollars)* Thanks.

JOHN   What did you think of that dance?

MACK   That was swinging, man.

JOHN   Was that swinging? Or wasn't that swinging?

MACK   That was swinging, man.

JOHN   Did you ever see anyone swing like that?

MACK   Not that I can remember.

JOHN   Try to remember.

MACK *thinks.*

Well? . . .

MACK   I can't remember.

JOHN   Try.

MACK   I said I can't remember.

JOHN   Then you never saw anyone swing like that.

MACK   I can't remember.

JOHN   If you can't remember it's because you never saw anyone swing like that.

MACK   I don't know.

JOHN   *(Twisting* MACK's *arm)* What do you mean, you don't know?

MACK   I don't know.

JOHN   If you had, you would remember.

MACK *doesn't answer.* JOHN *points his gun at* MACK's *temple.*

If you had, you would remember.

MACK   I suppose.

JOHN   Don't suppose. Did you or didn't you?

MACK   No, I never did.

JOHN   *(In narcissistic rapture)* Ahhhhhhh.

MACK   Jesus! What a creep.

JOHN   Ask that lady in.

MACK   What lady?

JOHN   The one you turned out.

MACK   The child?

JOHN   Ask her in.

MACK   Jesus!

Lights go back to normal. MACK *goes to the door. On his way there* HE *stops by* JIM*'s table and gives him back his dollar.*

MOLLY   *(To* JOHN*)* If that's your taste you don't belong in my book of names and telephones like a sailor. . . . I cross you out.

JOHN   What is she talking about?

MOLLY   If you like her.

MACK   Don't pay any attention to her.

JIM   Can't even speak English.

MOLLY   I can when I want to. . . . I only don't want to.

MACK   *(To* ALBERTA*)* All right. You can come in.

ALBERTA *dances in.*

JIM   You know why you haven't grown?

JOHN   She's grown.

ALBERTA   Why?

JIM   Because you haven't been loved.

ALBERTA   Creep.

JIM   I thought you might want to know.

ALBERTA   No, I don't want to know. I am a child. That's why I haven't grown. And I get plenty of love, so leave me alone.

JIM   How old are you?

ALBERTA   Twenty-seven.

JIM   *(HE considers a moment)* You need love.

JOHN   The lady is with me if you don't mind.

JIM   No, I don't mind. But she should mind.

JOHN   Why should she mind?

ALBERTA   I don't mind.

   JOHN *presses* ALBERTA*'s hand against his lips and remains in that position until* HE *speaks again.*

JIM   *(To* ALBERTA*)* You need love.

   ALBERTA *makes an obscene gesture to* JIM.

MACK   *(Referring to* JIM*)* Boy, he's finished.

JIM   What do you expect? You get involved with a broad like that and you're cooked. I didn't know she was German.

MOLLY   I was not German. I became German. You made me become German.

JIM   You always had it in you.

MOLLY   I am not a hen. I will not share my rooster with other hens. I'm the only hen or I'm not a hen.

JIM   She's crazy.

MOLLY   I may be crazy but I'm not a hen.

JIM   What's wrong with hens?

MOLLY   There's nothing wrong with hens. Only I'm not a hen.

JIM   I don't see why you had to be the only one. The others were happy.

MOLLY   But I'm not happy.

JIM   She's crazy.

MOLLY   I'm just wise and tough about you men.

JIM   I don't like tough women. I'm through with you.

MOLLY   I'm through with you before you are through with me.

JIM   Can't even speak English.

MOLLY   Only when I get angry. (SHE goes to the bird cage and sets the bird free) Fly away mine kleiner Vogel, baby. *Esse alle Würmer die du kannst*. That means: fly away my little bird. Eat all the worms you can. Fly away mine kleiner Vogel, baby. *Esse alle Würmer die du kannst*.

The HANGING WOMEN *surround* MOLLY.

No . . . no . . . no . . .

The HANGING WOMEN *giggle and go back to their places.*

JIM   Creep.

MOLLY   Little man.

JIM *goes to* JOHN *and* ALBERTA.

MACK   His pride is hurt.

JIM   No, it is not. I just think there's something wrong with her.
   (To JOHN *and* ALBERTA*)* May I join you?

JOHN   If the lady wishes.

ALBERTA   All right. But don't tell me I'm a hen.

JIM   I never told you you were a hen.

ALBERTA   I mean, OK, but don't tell me I need love.

JIM   OK. *(HE sits)*

JOHN   Madam? . . .

ALBERTA   Sir? . . .

JOHN   Would you like anything to drink?

ALBERTA   I'll have a mint julep with cherry syrup.

JOHN   *(To* JIM*)* Would your lady friend like a drink?

JIM   I have no lady friend. Can't you see I have no lady friend?
   (HE gives MOLLY *a dirty look)*

ALBERTA   You don't have to get rude. You have no lady friend
   because you have no manners.

JOHN   *(To the* HANGING WOMAN*)* Would you like a drink, madam?

   The HANGING WOMAN *smiles.*

JIM   Why aren't you with the others?

The HANGING WOMAN *joins the* OTHERS.

Creep!

JOHN *(To* MACK*)* A mint julep with cherry syrup. . . . Make it two.

JIM See? He's not real. He just drinks what everybody else drinks.

ALBERTA I still like him better than you. Even if he's not real.

JOHN I'm real. Can't you see I'm real? *(*HE *pinches himself and shakes the table)* Could I have done that if I weren't real?

ALBERTA You're real. It's he who is not real.

JOHN *presses* ALBERTA*'s hand against his lips.*

JIM *(Dismissing the subject)* I'm real.

ALBERTA *(Referring to* JOHN*)* And besides being real, he's cute.

JOHN My peach. *(*HE *presses her hand against his lips again)*

JIM You see what I mean? He's not real.

ALBERTA He looks real to me.

JOHN My peach . . . my pearl . . . *(*HE *presses* ALBERTA*'s hand against his lips)*

JIM He's just pretending to be real. That's why he kisses you.

ALBERTA *(Hitting* JIM *on the head)* He's not pretending. He kisses me because he likes my baby flesh . . . and you stop bothering us. We want to be alone. Sit somewhere else.

JOHN My peach, my pearl, my persimmon, I want to be alone with you. My peach, my pearl, when the impossible begins to seem possible. When love knocks at our door. All our expectations, dreams, desires go rampant. There is no end to what seems possible. There is no end to what we ask for. Sugar baby, candy child, give me your life.

ALBERTA   *(Matter-of-fact)* No.

JOHN *picks* ALBERTA *up.* HE *looks for a place to take her.* HE *is like a wild beast looking for a place to take his prey.* SHE *gets away from him.* HE *runs after her.*

HANGING WOMEN   *(Sing)*

Is this true passion,
Or the way a vain man has
Of saying to himself:
I am not dead?

JOHN

I am not dead.
Not dead.
Not dead.

HANGING WOMEN

Is this true love?
True love?
True love?

One very long,
Very narrow,
Very old idea.
An old idea.
A long idea.
An old, old,
Withered idea,
Without reward.

A withering idea.
One very narrow,
Very old idea.
A narrow idea.

ALBERTA   Me, the little darling. The heaven on earth. The night
without pain. The honey of the flowers. I will not be yours. Ever.
. . . I can't. . . . I'm pure.

JOHN   My fairy tale, my peach, my pearl, grant me my wish.

ALBERTA   No.

JOHN   I am in control of my emotions. I always have been. Once I
was almost in love. Yes, indeed, no one can say I've never loved.
I am an important man. My scope is very narrow. Yes, it's very
narrow, but it is wide enough to strike a pose of self-importance.
. . . That's all I need. . . . Me, a failure? Never! I'm in control
of my emotions. My emotions are feeble. Me, strong. The more
I'm known to strangers the more I lose my sense of dignity. I
have no point of view. I am well known, that's all I need. You
know me. I know myself. What, me, get old? Never! That's not
for me. Candy child, give me your life.

ALBERTA   No.

JOHN *moves behind* ALBERTA *and sinks his teeth into her neck.
Through the following song* JOHN *and* ALBERTA *take vampirical
love-making poses. Between the poses, and with the aid of the*
HANGING WOMEN, THEY *do a costume change with rapid choreographed movements.* JOHN *removes his guns and his hat and puts
on a cape.* ALBERTA *takes her wig off, letting her hair loose. Her
dress grows long to the floor.* HE *looks like a vampire.* SHE *is
sensuous and glamorous.* HE *sinks his teeth into her neck again.*

HANGING WOMEN   *(Sing)*

Is this true passion,
Or the way a vain man has

Of saying to himself:
I am not dead?

Is this true love?
True love?
True love?

HE *lifts his head and looks around.* HE *moves in front of her and stretches his arms as if to protect her.*

JOHN   Don't anyone touch my own. She's mine.

JIM   Who wants to.

JOHN   My one and only. My own.

MACK   Creep.

JOHN   Ahhh. Love, love, love . . . *(*HE *does a pirouette)* I feel at last alive.

HE *dances around with movements resembling a lizard's.* HE *then takes* ALBERTA *to the mirror. By means of rear projection one sees* ALBERTA *in the mirror but not* JOHN. HE *moves away from her in terror and shame.*

JOHN   *(To* ALBERTA, *from a distance)* Tell me that you see me.

SHE *takes a step back.*

Tell me that you love me.

SHE *looks away from him.*

Kiss me.

JOHN   Ahhh. My love recoils from me.

HE *sits down at a table.* HE *is downcast.* ALBERTA *takes two steps toward him but stops.* HE *watches her.*

My lady said the hair around my temple
Is different from the rest,
And that it is a sight to behold.
She said it is smooth and grows downward,
While the rest grows wild.

My lady said there's a line
From the back of my ear to my shoulder
That gives her pleasure to look at.
And she said as a present
She'll give me a flock of birds.
She is my love.
That lady is my love.

She speaks of love
Only angels know,
And yet she fears me.
My lady fears me.

SHE *moves toward him.*

My lady said
The joint that holds my jaw to my skull
Is delicate like a bird's.
So my lady said.

My lady said my face is life itself.
She is my love.
That lady is my love,
And yet, she fears me.

My lady said when she held me in her arms
She held not a man but the world.
And yet my lady fears me.
She fears me.

ALBERTA *goes to* JOHN. SHE *brings her hand to his cheek and kisses him.*

ALBERTA *(Sings)*

The senses are five:
Sight, smell, hearing, taste, touch.
Los sentidos. Les sens. I sentiti.
The verb to sense in French
Refers to smelling, *"sens."*
Tu sens bon.
In Italian, *"sentire,"*
It refers to hearing.
Sente amore mio.
In Spanish, *"sentir,"*
It means to feel.
Siento en la alma
Unas ganas intensas de llorar.
In English to sense
Is nothing you can put your finger on.
I sense something unusual all around me.

Love, love, love. Love, love, love, love.
You have brought me to my senses
You have made sense of me
And the sense of me is you.
I hear. I see. I smell. I taste. I touch.
Oh, love.
My life is senseless without you.

THEY *kiss. His back is to the audience. A cape* HE *wears rolled up around his neck is let down. The cape bears an "S."* JOHN *is now* SUPERMAN. HE *turns around. An "S" is visible on his chest.* THEY *circle around the stage as if strolling in the park. The* HANGING WOMEN *surround them singing. When* THEY *reach the center of the stage* THEY *each circle the stage in opposite directions.* HALF *the* HANGING WOMEN *follow* JOHN, *the* OTHER HALF *follow* ALBERTA. *They meet in the center again, and walk down the aisle, followed by the* HANGING WOMEN *who carry garlands.*

HANGING WOMEN *(Sing)*

> She is my love.
> That lady is my love.
> She speaks of love
> Only angels know.

MACK   Molly, that kid is doing better than you.

MOLLY   No, she is not.

MACK   Yes, she is.

HANGING WOMEN

> She is my love.
> That lady is my love.
> She speaks of love
> Only angels know.

THEY *exit.*

JIM   Fiddlesticks.

There is a short pause and a sense of sadness.

Yeah, that's how it is.

MOLLY   Mack, play something amusing, Sam. I feel sad.

THEY *are silent for a moment.* MOLLY *sighs.*

JIM   I beg your pardon?

MOLLY   Hm.

JIM   A second chance?

MOLLY   Hm.

JIM   Hm, hm. Not me. I'm quitting. . . . You had your chance.

THEY *recite the following:*

MOLLY

> To tell you I still love you?
> Why? You care?
> I loved you once.
> What? You think that's nothing?
> It isn't everyone who's loved the way I loved you.
> You're feeling sorry now.
> Well, too late, I'm quitting.
> You can't expect me to survive all that.

JIM

> I'm too proud. You're right.
> And you're a two-time loser.
> Once you had my love and didn't take it.
> That makes it once you were the loser.
> And now you want me back.
> You lose again.
> I'm too proud, you're right.
> I'm quitting.
> I'm not expected to survive all that.

JIM *walks to the door.* HE *and* MOLLY *start singing with their backs to each other.*

JIM AND MOLLY

> A sense of incompletion . . . yeah . . . yeah . . .
> A joke without a laugh,

A friend who doesn't hear,
A promise without hope,
An offer withdrawn,
A good-bye with no departure.
And what? Am I expected to survive all that?
Ha ha. Fat chance. Not me. I'm quitting.

JIM

Johnny told me, August first,
There'll be a parade.
Ha ha. If the city permits.

MOLLY

Ronnie told me, August second,
We'll see a movie.
Ha ha. He changed his mind.

JIM

My horoscope said, August third,
I'd have good news.
Ha ha. There was no news.

MOLLY

Mack told me, August fourth,
He'd give me a raise.
Ha ha. There was no raise.

JIM

My cousin told me, August fifth,
We'd go for a ride.
Ha ha. The car broke down.

MOLLY

    August sixth, I took the bus.
    It was a long ride,
    And when I got there,
    No one said hello.

JIM AND MOLLY

    And what? Am I expected to survive all that?
    Ha, ha. That's all I can say.
    Ha ha. Ha ha. Ha ha.

    JIM *walks to the door.* HE *turns back and shakes hands with* MOLLY.

JIM   Good-bye.

MOLLY   Good-bye.

    HE *walks to the door again.*

    You know . . .

JIM   . . . What? . . .

MOLLY   In order to become what we are . . .

JIM   Yes? . . .

MOLLY   We have to go through many stages.

JIM   Yes.

    MOLLY *puts on the top hat.* THEY *laugh.*

MOLLY   If we had met some other time . . . perhaps . . .

JIM   Perhaps we'll meet again some other time.

MOLLY   Yes.

JIM   I'll be going now. *(HE walks to the door)* See you later . . .
Molly?

MOLLY   *(Taking the hat off)* Yes . . .

JIM   You'll wait for me?

MOLLY   I will. . . . Will you recognize me?

JIM   Yes, I'll know you.

> THEY *wave.* HE *exits.* MOLLY *walks to the table where* SHE *first
> fell asleep.* SHE *leans her head on the table.* MACK *walks in and
> straightens the place, leaving it as in the beginning of the play.
> The* YOUNG MAN *enters.* HE *carries luggage which resembles in
> color the* HANGING WOMEN*'s costumes.* HE *looks at* MOLLY.

MACK   She's lost to the world. What would you have?

YOUNG MAN   Do you rent rooms?

MACK   No, we don't rent rooms.

YOUNG MAN   *(Picking up the luggage)* Oh, well . . .

> *The lights flash on and off. The* YOUNG MAN *puts the luggage
> down and turns to look at* MOLLY.

On second thought, I think I'll have a drink.

MACK   What would you like?

YOUNG MAN   Double rye.

MACK *pours the drink. The* YOUNG MAN *pays* MACK *and takes the drink to a table.*

I'll give my feet a rest. I walked from the station.

MACK *exits. The* YOUNG MAN *watches* MOLLY. HE *drinks his drink, takes a deep breath, picks up his bags, and exits. The lights fade except for a blue spot on* MOLLY's *head.* SHE *wakes up suddenly and looks where the* YOUNG MAN *sat. The spot is held for a few seconds while two high musical notes play. The spot fades.*

TANGO PALACE

To the memory of my father

Carlos Fornés 1891–1945

Tango Palace was first presented by the San Francisco
Actors Workshop at the Encore Theatre in San Francisco
on November 29, 1963, under the title *There! You Died.* It
was directed by Herbert Blau, with scene design and
costumes by Judith Davis, lighting by Dan Dugan, and the
following cast:

Isidore   *Robert Benson*
Leopold   *Dan Sullivan*

Tango Palace was subsequently presented at the Firehouse
Theatre in Minneapolis, in a production underwritten by
the University of Minnesota's Office of Advanced Drama
Research, on January 22, 1965, in a revised version. This
production was directed by Charles M. Morrison III and
designed by Marlow Hotchkiss, with the following cast:

Isidore   *Lionel Reid*
Leopold   *Michael Devine*

ISIDORE, an androgynous clown
LEOPOLD, an earnest youth

SCENE: A room, the same throughout the play. The floor is carpeted. The door is bolted with an oversize padlock. There is a big filing cabinet, an armchair, a secretary, a wall mirror, a water jug, a radio, three porcelain teapots, a large vase, a blackboard. There is a large canvas sack on the floor. A recess in the back wall serves as a shrine. Within the recess, hanging from nails, are a guitar, a whip, a toy parrot, a Persian helmet, two swords, a cape, a compass, a muleta, a pair of bulls horns, six banderillas, two masks in the form of beetles' faces. The shrine is decorated with a string of flower-shaped lightbulbs. ISIDORE sits in the shrine. His appearance is a mixture of man and woman. HE is stout, has long hair, and is wearing rouge and lipstick; HE wears a man's hat and pants, high-heeled shoes, and a silk blouse. There is a corsage of flowers pinned on his shirt. Sometimes his behavior is clearly masculine; other times HE could be thought a woman. LEOPOLD is inside the canvas sack. HE is in his late twenties. HE is handsome, and his movements are simple. HE wears a business suit. Each time ISIDORE feels HE has said something important, HE takes a card from his pocket or from a drawer and flips it across the room in any direction. (The word "card" in the script indicates when a card should be flipped.) This action is automatic.

SCENE 1

ISIDORE *makes a gesture and his shrine is lit.* HE *makes another gesture and chimes sound. One more gesture and the bulbs on his shrine light up.* LEOPOLD *begins to move inside the canvas sack.* ISIDORE *notices the sack and cautiously approaches it.*

ISIDORE Look what the stork has brought me.

ISIDORE *opens the sack.* LEOPOLD *begins to emerge.* THEY *stare at each other for a while.* ISIDORE *is delighted with what* HE *has found.* HE *goes to the shrine, takes the guitar and begins to sing "A Sleepy Lagoon" in an attempt to charm* LEOPOLD.

Song and guitar accompaniment by Isidore. *(Card)*

LEOPOLD *has gotten out of the sack and walks curiously about the room.* HE *stops in front of the armchair.* ISIDORE, *noticing* LEOPOLD'*s interest in the furniture, addresses him in the affected tones of a salesman in an exclusive shop.*

Queen Anne walnut armchair. Representing the acme of artistic craftsmanship of the Philadelphia school. Circa 1740. Original condition and finish. *(Card)*

ISIDORE *steps down from the shrine, walks ostentatiously past* LEOPOLD, *and runs his hand along the surface of the secretary.*

Very rare, small, Louis-Quinze secretary, representing the acme of artistic craftsmanship of the Parisian school. A pure Louis-Quinze leg was never, under any conditions, straight. It was always curvilinear, generally in that shaping which we have come to know as the "cabriole." *(Card. Taking little steps to the mirror)* Louis-Quatorze carved and gilded mirror. *(Card)* Bearing sprays of leafage and flowers. Circa 1700. Height sixty-four inches. Width thirty-six inches.

ISIDORE *walks close to* LEOPOLD *and looks him over.*

The choice of the examples here is influenced by their significance as distinct types representative of the best tradition, not only in the style and execution but in the choice of subject. *(Card.* ISIDORE *walks toward the shelf containing the porcelain objects)* Teapots of rarest Chinese export porcelain with American marine decoration. Circa 1740–1750. Left one shows American Flag, right one American admiral's insignia. The one in the center depicts the so-called "Governor Duff," actually

Diedrick Durven, Governor-general of the Dutch East India Company. Exquisite, isn't it? This collection has been formed throughout a period of many years, and it is probably not an exaggeration to say that such a collection could not be formed again. *(Waiting for a reaction)* Did you say something? . . . Oh, well . . . Listen . . . Music . . . A tango . . . *(Card.* ISIDORE *begins to dance)* Do you know this step? Stomach in. Derrière out. Fingers gracefully curved. *(Card)* A smile on your lips. Eyes full of stars. Dancing has well been called the poetry of motion. It is the art whereby the feelings of the mind are expressed by measured steps, regulated motions of the body, and graceful gestures. The German waltz, the Spanish fandango, the Polish mazurka, and last but not least the Argentine tango. One . . . two . . . three . . . dip and turn your head to show your profile. One . . . two . . . three . . . dip and swing your little foot back and forth.

LEOPOLD *begins to imitate* ISIDORE.

One . . . two . . . three . . . and rotate on one foot, taking little steps with the other. Watch me first. Now you made me lose my step. And a one and a two and a three. Stomach in. Derrière out. Fingers gracefully curved. A smile on your lips. Eyes full of stars. One . . . two . . . three . . . dip and profile. One . . . two . . . three . . . and rotate.

LEOPOLD *'s attention is drawn by the shrine;* HE *moves closer to it.*

Don't look there yet. Watch me . . . watch me.

LEOPOLD *watches for a moment, then* HE *turns to the shrine again and reaches for the whip.* ISIDORE *takes the whip and demonstrates its use.*

This is my whip. *(Lashing* LEOPOLD*)* And that is pain. *(Card)* A souvenir of love. I loved her. She loved me. I gave her the whip. She gave me her cherry . . . All is fair in love and war.

(Card. Taking the parrot) This is my talking parrot. *(To the Parrot)* Pretty parrot.

PARROT Pretty parrot.

ISIDORE Very smart. He knows everything.

PARROT Very smart. He knows everything.

ISIDORE Thank you.

PARROT Thank you.

ISIDORE *(Putting on the Persian helmet)* And this is the genuine Persian helmet I wore when I fought at Salamis. *(Card)* I killed two hundred and fifteen Athenians. Fourteen were captains, three were generals, and the rest foot soldiers. I'll show you.

ISIDORE *takes the sword and swings it while* HE *screams, grunts, whirls, and hops.* LEOPOLD *becomes frightened.*

That's how I killed them. Don't be afraid, I won't hurt you. *(Touching* LEOPOLD*'s chest with the tip of the sword)* Do you have something to show me?

LEOPOLD No. I don't have anything.

ISIDORE Nothing at all?

LEOPOLD No.

ISIDORE Oh, that's too bad. Here, I'll show you my flying cape.

ISIDORE *puts on the cape, climbs on a chair, flips his arms, and jumps to the floor.*

Extraordinary, isn't it? Would you like to see my joy compass? *(Showing joy compass)* It's magic. I sent for it . . . it points to joy. Now you show me something.

LEOPOLD   I don't own anything.

ISIDORE   Were your things taken away?

LEOPOLD   No, I never had anything, except . . .

ISIDORE   What?

LEOPOLD   A tattoo. *(HE opens his shirt)*

ISIDORE   Oh, how beautiful. *(Reading)* "This is man. Heaven or
bust." Oh, that's in bad taste. That's in terrible taste. *(Card)*
Just for that you can't touch any of my things. The only
things you can touch are those cards. Those cards are yours.
(Card)

LEOPOLD   *(Picking up a card)* These cards are mine? *(Reading)* "A
tattoo." "Oh. How beautiful. This is man. Heaven or bust. Oh,
that's in bad taste."

ISIDORE   You can put them there in that filing cabinet.

LEOPOLD   *(Disturbed)* Why do you write what I say?

ISIDORE   First of all, I write what *we* say. And then I don't write.
I print . . . with my magic printing press . . . if you'd like to know.
File them in your filing cabinet. That cabinet is yours too.

LEOPOLD   What for?

ISIDORE   So you can find them when you need them. These cards
contain wisdom. File them away. *(Card)* Know where they are.
(Card) Have them at hand. *(Card)* Be one upon whom nothing
is lost. *(Card)* Memorize them and you'll be where you were.
(Card) Be where you are. Then and now. Pick them up.

LEOPOLD   *(Reading a card)* "All is fair in love and war."

ISIDORE   That's a good one.

LEOPOLD   Why?

ISIDORE   Because it teaches you that all is fair in love and war, and it teaches you that when someone is telling you a story about love and war, you are not to stand there and say . . . That's not fair . . . or you'll be considered a perfect fool. *(Card)*

LEOPOLD   *(Still disturbed)* I don't see why love in war should be different from love in anything else.

ISIDORE   *(Pulling* LEOPOLD *'s ear and shouting)* Not love *in* war. Love *and* war! It has taken centuries . . . *(Smack)* Centuries, to arrive at this ethical insight and you say it isn't fair. *(Smack)* All is fair. You hear? All is fair in love . . . *(Smack)* and war. *(Smack)*

LEOPOLD   I don't want your cards. I don't want to have anything to do with them.

ISIDORE   These are not my cards. They are yours. It's you who need learning, not me. I've learned already. *(Card)* I know all my cards by heart. *(Card)* I can recite them in chronological order and I don't leave one word out. *(Card)* What's more I never say a thing which is not an exact quotation from one of my cards. *(Card)* That's why I never hesitate. *(Card)* Why I'm never short of an answer. *(Card)* Or a question. *(Card)* Or a remark, if a remark is more appropriate.

LEOPOLD   I don't want to learn that way.

ISIDORE   There is no other way.

LEOPOLD   Yes, there is. I hear a voice.

ISIDORE   What voice? That's me you hear. I am the only voice.

LEOPOLD   No, it's not you.

ISIDORE   It is so. *(In a falsetto voice)* Listen to me and always obey me . . . It's me . . . me . . . It's me . . . and only me . . . Leopold . . . Lippy . . . *me . . . me . . .*

LEOPOLD   No.

ISIDORE   Well, *Dime con quien andas y te dire quien eres . . . (Card)* Spanish proverb meaning . . . You know what it means, and if you don't, go and ask that voice of yours . . . What does your voice say?

LEOPOLD   You speak like a parrot.

ISIDORE   No, I don't. *(Isidore considers for a moment)* My diction is better. Sally says she sells sea shells at the seashore. Have you ever heard a parrot say: Sally says she sells sea shells at the seashore?

LEOPOLD   That's not what I mean.

ISIDORE   *(Considers for a moment)* I talk like a wise parrot. Study hard, learn your cards, and one day, you too will be able to talk like a parrot.

LEOPOLD   *(Imitating a parrot)* Study hard, learn your cards and one day, you too will be able to talk like a parrot.

ISIDORE   What are you, a parrot? Do you want to be a moron for the rest of your life? Always being pushed around?

ISIDORE *pushes* LEOPOLD.

Are you mentally retarded? Do I have to tell you what should be obvious to a half-wit? *(Smack)* It should be obvious *(Smack)* even *(Smack)* to a half-wit?

LEOPOLD *throws a punch at* ISIDORE. ISIDORE *ducks, and kicks* LEOPOLD. LEOPOLD *falls.* ISIDORE *turns and thrusts his buttocks out.*

You bad, bad boy. You'll have to be punished. You tried to hit your loving teacher. Come.

ISIDORE *picks* LEOPOLD *up.*

LEOPOLD *(Freeing himself from* ISIDORE*)* Take your hands off me.

LEOPOLD *executes each of* ISIDORE*'s commands at the same time as it is spoken, but as if* HE *were acting spontaneously rather than obeying.*

ISIDORE   Walk to the door. *(Card)* Notice the padlock. *(Card)* Push the door. *(Card)* You're locked in. *(Card)* Stand there and think. *(Card)* Why are you locked in? *(Card)* Where are you locked in? *(Card)* Turn to the door. *(Card)* You know what to do. *(Card)* Pull the padlock. *(Card)* Push the door. *(Card)* Force the padlock. *(Card)* You are locked in. *(Card)* Kick the door. *(Card)* Bang the door. *(Card)* Scream.

ISIDORE and LEOPOLD   Anybody there! Anybody there! *(Card)* Let me out. *(Card)* Open up! *(Card)*

ISIDORE   Kick the door. *(Card)* Walk around the room restlessly. *(Card)* Bite your thumbnails. *(Card)* Get an idea. *(Card)* You got an idea. *(Card)*

LEOPOLD *charges toward* ISIDORE.

Violence does not pay. *(Card)* Be sensible, stand still a moment being sensible. Have sensible thoughts. For every door there's a key. *(Card)* The key must be in the room. Look for it in the obvious place first. Under the rare seventeenth-century needle-work carpet depicting Elijah in the desert fed by ravens. It's not there. Look in Louis Quinze secretary, mahogany wood. Look in less obvious places. Magnificent marked Wedgwood vase in Rosso Antico ground. In flyleaf of my Gutenberg Bible. Look in places which are not obvious at all. Correction. All places are obvious places. *(Card)* Look again in drawer of very rare, small, Louis Quinze secretary, representing the acme of artistic craftsmanship. Fall exhausted on Queen Anne chair. Have desperate thoughts.

LEOPOLD *kicks the chair.* ISIDORE *speaks soothingly, to regain control.*

Collect yourself, darling. You must collect yourself.

LEOPOLD I must collect myself.

ISIDORE You must collect yourself. You must think, dear. Let's think. Could you have enemies? Perhaps business associates? Perhaps people who envy you? Or could it be the others? The angry husbands? The spinsters? The barking dogs? The man whose toilet you dirtied?

LEOPOLD Could it be you?

ISIDORE Could it be you? It doesn't really matter. You might as well stay. Just tidy up your things, darling. Do as I said. File them away.

LEOPOLD *(Picks up a card and reads it)* And that is pain.

ISIDORE Be where you were. *(Card)*

LEOPOLD *(Reading another card)* Pretty parrot. Very smart. He knows everything.

ISIDORE Then and now. *(Card)*

LEOPOLD *(Reading another card)* Were your things taken away?

ISIDORE   Nothing is lost. *(Card)*

LEOPOLD   Nothing is lost?

ISIDORE   Nothing. Come, it's time for your drawing lesson. *(ISIDORE rings the bell and walks to the blackboard to illustrate the lesson)* How to draw a portrait. *(Making a mark at the top of the blackboard)* This is the divine. Cleopatra, for example. *(Making a mark at the bottom of the blackboard)* This down here is the despicable. The werewolf. Now we're going to place the person whose portrait we're drawing. Where shall we put him? Close to the divine? Not so close. Halfway down? Close to the despicable? No. Here. *(ISIDORE makes a mark to the left and halfway between the other two marks)* Now you join the points with lines. This is the portrait of a mediocre person. You can draw a mouth on it. And an eye. But it isn't necessary. Because what counts is the nose.

The figure ISIDORE *has drawn looks like this:*

LEOPOLD   Draw my portrait.

ISIDORE   Unfortunately, this system doesn't do you any good, since all we can establish is that I am at the top. And way down at the bottom is you. There is no other point. We therefore can't have an angle. We only have a vertical line. The space around us is infinite, enclosed as it may be, because there is not a third person. And if the space around us is infinite, so is, necessarily, the space between us.

LEOPOLD   Who says you're at the top?

ISIDORE   I.

LEOPOLD   I say you're not at the top.

ISIDORE   But I am.

LEOPOLD   How do you know?

ISIDORE   Because I know everything. I know my cards. I know everything.

LEOPOLD   I'm going to burn those cards.

ISIDORE   You'll die if you burn them . . . don't take my word for it.
Try it.

   LEOPOLD *sets fire to a card.*

What in the world are you doing? Are you crazy?

   ISIDORE *puts the fire out.*

Are you out of your mind? You're going to die. Are you dying?
Do you feel awful?

   ISIDORE *trips* LEOPOLD.

There! You died.

LEOPOLD   *(Springing to his feet)* No, I tripped. I think I tripped.

ISIDORE   See? You tripped because you burned that card. If I hadn't
put the fire out you would have died.

LEOPOLD   I don't believe you.

ISIDORE   You don't believe me? You could have broken your neck. All right, I don't care what you think. You just stop burning things.

LEOPOLD   You're lying to me, aren't you?

ISIDORE   Go on, burn them if you want to. I won't stop you.

LEOPOLD *moves to burn a card but then stops himself.* ISIDORE *flips a card at* LEOPOLD.

Wisdom. *(Card.* ISIDORE *begins to dance)*

LEOPOLD   *(Holding* ISIDORE *to stop him from dancing)* I beg you.

ISIDORE   Don't put your hands on me, ever, ever, ever, ari, ari, ari. That's Bengali, you know. *(Card)* It's you who need learning. *(Card)* Very smart. He knows everything. *(Card)* A souvenir of love. She gave me her cherry. *(Card)* I killed two hundred and fifteen Athenians. *(Card)* That's a good one. *(Card)* A sleepy lagoon. *(Card)* What does your voice say? *(Card)*

LEOPOLD   Stop flipping those things at me . . . I beg you . . . Don't . . . Please . . . I beg you. *(Kneels at* ISIDORE*'s feet)*

ISIDORE   And a one and a two. One, two, three, dip and turn . . . You still have to be punished. Don't think I forgot.

ISIDORE *takes* LEOPOLD *by the hand and walks him to a corner.* LEOPOLD *leans against the wall.*

Straighten yourself up. Are you hearing things again? I'm jealous. I want to hear too. *(Putting his ear against* LEOPOLD*'s ear)* Where is it? I can't hear a thing. *(Talking into* LEOPOLD*'s ear)* Yoo hoo. Where are you? Say something. Talk to me. It won't talk to me. *(To* LEOPOLD*)* Tell me what it says. I'm angry.

ISIDORE *sits on the shrine, crosses his legs and his arms, and turns his head away from* LEOPOLD.

I'm angry. Don't talk to me. I said don't talk to me. Don't you see I'm in the typical position of anger? . . . Do you want to say something to me?

LEOPOLD   No.

ISIDORE   Well, I want you to tell me what that awful voice was telling you.

LEOPOLD   It said, "Isidore deceives you." It said, "Don't listen to Isidore."

ISIDORE   Oh, Horrible. Horrible. Treason in my own house.

LEOPOLD   Let me tell you . . .

ISIDORE   Oh, Don't say any more, treason. Oh.

LEOPOLD   Let me tell you what I think, Isidore.

ISIDORE   No.

LEOPOLD   Please.

ISIDORE   You've said enough.

LEOPOLD   I haven't said . . .

ISIDORE   Treason!

LEOPOLD   Isidore!

ISIDORE   *(In a whisper)* Don't talk so loud.

LEOPOLD   *(In a whisper)* I haven't said . . .

ISIDORE   I heard you already. Treason!

LEOPOLD   I want to leave.

ISIDORE   Bye, bye, butterfly.

LEOPOLD   I want to get out.

ISIDORE   See you later, alligator.

LEOPOLD   Give me the key.

ISIDORE   Pretty parrot.

LEOPOLD   I want the key.

ISIDORE   He wants the key.

PARROT   He wants the key.

ISIDORE   There is no key.

PARROT   No key.

LEOPOLD   You're lying.

ISIDORE   I always tell the truth. I worship truth and truth worships
me. Don't be so stubborn. There is no key.

LEOPOLD   There must be a key.

ISIDORE   I see what possesses you. It's faith!

LEOPOLD   So what?

ISIDORE   Faith is a disgusting thing. It's treacherous and destructive. Mountains are moved from place to place. You can't find them. I won't have any of that.

LEOPOLD   Well, I do have faith.

ISIDORE   Infidel. I'm too upset. I can't take any more of this. *(Covers his face)* It's the devil. I can't look at you. Tell me you'll give it up. Tell me you have no faith.

LEOPOLD   But I do.

ISIDORE   Well, I'm a mountain. *Move me.*

LEOPOLD   I know there is a way out because there have been moments when I have been away from here.

ISIDORE   That's not true. You get ten demerits for telling lies.

LEOPOLD   It is true. There are moments when you have just vanished . . .

ISIDORE   Vanished? I have never vanished.

LEOPOLD   I don't mean vanished . . . exactly . . . I mean there are moments when I've felt this is not all there is.

ISIDORE   What else is there?

LEOPOLD   Close your eyes . . . Imagine . . . that all is calm.

ISIDORE   I don't like playing childish games. I'm supposed to sit there imagining a field of orange blossoms and then you're going to pour a bucket of water on my head. Let me tell you, young man, that I played that game when I was five. Let me tell you that it was I who invented that game. And let me tell you that I didn't invent it to sit there like a fool and get the water on *my* head. I invented it to pour the water on the fool's head. Let me tell you that. You're not smart enough . . . not for old Izzy. *(Card)*

LEOPOLD   I wasn't going to throw water on you.

ISIDORE   You weren't? Hm . . . all right. Go on.

LEOPOLD   Don't imagine anything in particular. Don't imagine orange groves or anything. Make your mind a blank. Just imagine that you are in perfect harmony with everything around you . . .

ISIDORE   Wait, I have to erase the orange grove.

LEOPOLD   Forget about the orange grove.

ISIDORE   I can't forget the orange grove. It's planted in my mind. I have to uproot it. You put things in my mind and then it's I who have to get rid of them. At least leave me in peace for a moment, while I do the work.

LEOPOLD   I didn't put anything in your mind.

ISIDORE   You said, "Don't think of an orange grove." You did, didn't you?

LEOPOLD   Yes . . .

ISIDORE   Well, the moment you said that, an orange grove popped into my head. Now give me time while I get rid of it.

ISIDORE *moves about the room as if* HE *were picking up oranges and throwing them over a fence with his eyes closed.* LEOPOLD's *impatience increases.*

First I'll throw this orange over the fence. Then, this little orange. Then, this orange orange. Now this rotten orange. Now I pull this whole branch off the tree. Oh, oh, it's so hard. Now

I pull this orange off the tree. Oh, oh, there are so many. There are thousands and thousands and I think millions and trillions. Oh, I'm tired. No, no, I must not rest. I can't take a moment's rest until I clear away all this mess of oranges. Thousands and thousands of acres, and then I have to clear the other side of the fence, and then the other, and then the other and then dismantle the fence, and then the other fence, and then . . .

LEOPOLD *reaches for the pitcher of water and empties it on* ISIDORE. THEY *remain motionless for a moment.* ISIDORE *goes to his shrine and sits in his typical angry position.* LEOPOLD *walks to the opposite end of the room and sits down.*

I'll never trust you again.

The lights fade out. ISIDORE *laughs out loud as the curtain falls.*

SCENE 2

The curtain rises with ISIDORE *and* LEOPOLD *in the same position as at the end of the first scene.*

ISIDORE *(Sings)*

Isidore, I beg you
Have you no heart?
You play games,
And I'm so earnest.
Isidore, I beg you.
Can't you see
You're breaking my heart?
'Cause while I'm so earnest,
You're still playing games.

Sung and composed by Isidore. Sixteen years old. *(Card)*

LEOPOLD *looks at* ISIDORE.

Stop looking at me like that.

LEOPOLD   Like what?

ISIDORE   *(Accompanying himself on the guitar)* Like a lover. Transfigured by the presence of the beloved. Looking as though you want to breathe the minute bubbles of air imprisoned in each of my pores. *(Card)* Or like a drug addict who imagines specks of heroin concealed in those beloved dimples. *(Card)*

LEOPOLD   And you think that's how I'm looking at you, you slob?

ISIDORE   I'm offended. *(Pause)* Come and make up with old Isidore.

LEOPOLD   Leave me alone.

ISIDORE   You'd die of boredom if I left you alone . . . *(Pause)* You'd have to come to me sooner or later. Come now. *(Pause)* What if I don't take you later?

LEOPOLD   The better for me.

ISIDORE   I'll count up to ten.

LEOPOLD   Count up to ten.

ISIDORE   Don't be a stubborn brat.

LEOPOLD   Leave me alone.

ISIDORE   *(Takes the Persian helmet and sets it on* LEOPOLD*'s head)* I'll let you wear it for a while. There's my baby. Isn't he cute.

LEOPOLD *takes the helmet off.*

See how contradictory you are? When I wouldn't lend it to you, you wanted it. Now that I'm willing to lend it to you, you don't want it.

LEOPOLD   Oh, go to hell. You twist everything.

ISIDORE   Now you're being rude.

LEOPOLD   Go back to your hole.

LEOPOLD *picks up some cards and begins to sort them.*

ISIDORE   My hole. My hole? *(ISIDORE looks through his cards)* He means my shrine. I think I will. *(ISIDORE goes to the shrine doing a dance step)* Peekaboo.

LEOPOLD *stands in front of* ISIDORE.

LEOPOLD   Listen to me.

ISIDORE   Yes.

LEOPOLD   You're going to start behaving from now on.

ISIDORE *nods in consent.*

O.K. That's all.

LEOPOLD *goes back to the cards.* ISIDORE *passes wind through his lips.*

ISIDORE   So I'm going to start behaving from now on. Then what? . . . Stop being silly. What is the matter with you, young man? You should be ashamed of yourself. What is life without humor here and there? A little bit of humor . . . Look at him sorting out his little cards. He's a good boy.

LEOPOLD   I'm not sorting them. I just don't want to listen to you.

ISIDORE   You can't tear yourself away from them. Can you? . . . You think I haven't seen you running to your cards the moment you think I'm not looking?

LEOPOLD   That's a lie. I've never . . .

ISIDORE   I never lie. I have never lied in my life. *(Card.* ISIDORE *crosses himself, then covers his head as if to protect himself from lightning.)* So what if I'm a liar. Do you think truth matters? Well, it doesn't. *(Card)* Does that confound your infantile mind? It is order that matters, whether there's order or disorder. *(Card)* A sloppy liar is despicable, *(Card)* as despicable as a sloppy truth-teller. *(Card)* Now, what do you deduce from that?

LEOPOLD   That you're rotten.

LEOPOLD *flips a card to* ISIDORE. ISIDORE *sniffs himself.*

ISIDORE   A systematic liar, a man with a goal, a man with a style is the best sort. *(Card)* The most reliable. You'll never amount to anything until you learn that. No, you'll never amount to anything. You'll never make it in the army, the navy, politics, business, stardom. You're worthless. I'm almost tempted to give you the key.

LEOPOLD   Give it to me.

ISIDORE   Never mind that. Come here. I'm about to forgive you . . . Come now. You really don't want me to forgive you?

LEOPOLD   Where is it, Isidore?

ISIDORE   Oh, here, in my heart.

LEOPOLD   Where is it?

ISIDORE   Oh, you're so insistent. I'll tell you what. *(*ISIDORE *takes the horns and the cape)* I'll answer all the questions you want if you do a little thing for me. Be a good bull and charge. Then I'll answer your question.

LEOPOLD   You'll tell me where the key is?

ISIDORE   Yes. Charge six times and I'll give you the key. . . . But you won't be satisfied with the key. On the contrary, it's when you have the key that you'll start asking questions. You'll start wondering about the mysteries of the universe. *(Counting the banderillas)* One, two, three, four, five, six mysteries has the universe. As I stick each banderilla in your back I'll reveal the answer to a mystery. And then *(Taking the sword)* the moment of truth. Right through the back of your neck. Oh, beautiful transgressions. While I'm answering your last question you'll be expiring your last breath. As eternal verity is revealed to you, darkness will come upon your eyes . . . Fair? Fair. Charge.

LEOPOLD   Are you kidding?

ISIDORE   I am not kidding. I am proposing the most poetic diversion ever enjoyed by man. You mean to say you're not willing to die for the truth? *(*ISIDORE *rubs his fingers to indicate "shame")*

LEOPOLD   And when I'm crawling and bleeding to death begging you to answer my questions you'll say something like . . . Ha ha.

ISIDORE   You want to play or you don't want to play?

LEOPOLD   I'll play. But I'll only charge six times. Six passes. I only want one answer. No mysteries.

ISIDORE   All right. Ask your question.

LEOPOLD   Where is the key?

ISIDORE   Charge.

LEOPOLD   Answer first.

ISIDORE   The answer after you charge.

LEOPOLD *begins to charge.*

Wait. I lost the mood. I need preparation.

ISIDORE *kneels in front of the shrine and crosses himself.* HE *makes a trumpet with his hand and toots a bullfighter's march.* ISIDORE *performs the passes as* HE *calls out the passes' names.*

Toro and bull. Fearless, confident and dominant, without altering the composure of his figure. Isidore lifts the spectators from their seats as he receives his enemy with *Veronica.*

LEOPOLD   One.

ISIDORE   *(Turns his back toward the audience)* Turning his back to the planks below the box occupied by the Isidore Fan Club to whom he has dedicated this bull. He performs a dangerous *Revolera.* Marvelous both in its planning and development.

LEOPOLD   Two.

ISIDORE   *Faroles.* And the embellishment.

LEOPOLD   Four.

ISIDORE   Three. A punishing pass. *Pase de castigo.* All of Isidore's passes have identical depth and majestic sobriety.

LEOPOLD   Four.

ISIDORE   *Manoletina.* Astounding elegance and smoothness. The music breaks out and competes with the deafening clamor of the multitude.

LEOPOLD   Five.

ISIDORE *bows,* LEOPOLD *charges.*

ISIDORE Then, with authentic domination, he performs the *Isidorina.*

ISIDORE *circles the stage and bows.*

Ovation. One ear, turn. And cheers.

LEOPOLD Six. Answer.

ISIDORE Gore me.

LEOPOLD Answer.

ISIDORE Gore me. That's the answer.

LEOPOLD *charges against* ISIDORE, *this time determined to get him.* ISIDORE *avoids him with a banderillero's turn while* HE *thrusts a banderilla into* LEOPOLD's *back.*

Saint Sebastian!

LEOPOLD *falls to the floor.* ISIDORE *kneels beside him and holds him in his arms.*

Good bull. He attacked nobly and bravely. His killer made him take fifty-one passes and he would have continued charging, following docilely the course marked by deceit. He was cheered as he was hauled out, but less than he deserved.

ISIDORE *pulls out the banderilla from* LEOPOLD's *back and caresses him tenderly.* LEOPOLD *looks at* ISIDORE *imploringly.* ISIDORE *kisses* LEOPOLD.

I have no alternative.

LEOPOLD   Don't tell me that, Isidore. I can't believe that.

ISIDORE   I have no alternative, Leopold.

LEOPOLD   No alternative? The alternative is simple.

ISIDORE   It isn't simple. I can't be good to you.

LEOPOLD   Just try.

ISIDORE   It's not within my power.

LEOPOLD   Have you no will then?

ISIDORE   No, I don't will it.

LEOPOLD   Who wills it?

ISIDORE   You, Leopold.

LEOPOLD   Me? It is not me, Isidore. You can't be right.

ISIDORE   It is you, Leopold.

LEOPOLD   I have never provoked you. I have never wished for anything but kindness from you. I have never tried but for your love.

ISIDORE   Yes, and maybe it is just that. Maybe you have been too
patient, too good-natured.

LEOPOLD *is astounded. There is a moment's pause.* HE *then
struggles with* ISIDORE *to break from his embrace.*

LEOPOLD   You are rotten . . . What are you? What are you that you
must have rottenness around you? I am too patient? Too good-
natured? I will not become rotten for you. I will not become
rotten for you.

LEOPOLD *holds* ISIDORE *by the neck and tries to strangle him.*

ISIDORE   *(Gasping for air)* Son . . . son . . . let me tell you . . . let me tell you . . . a story . . . There was once a man . . . who . . .

LEOPOLD *covers his ears.*

It's very important. You must listen. There was once a man whose only companion was a white rat. He loved this white rat dearly. And one day the rat disappeared. The rat couldn't have left the room, because there were no doors, or windows, or even cracks on the walls or floor. Then the man, thinking that the rat could have hidden in some nook or cranny unknown to him, took his axe and wrecked everything he owned . . . The rat was nowhere in the room. He then turned to a picture of the rat which was hanging on the wall, and was about to wield his axe against it . . . but he stopped himself . . . He said, "This is the only thing I have left of my rat. If I destroy the picture, I will have nothing to remind me of him." And from that moment on, he began to speak to the picture of the rat and to caress it, and even feed it. Eventually, though, his loneliness brought him to such a state of melancholia that he no longer cared whether he was happy or not. He did not even care whether he lived or died. And as if he were summoning his own death, he picked up his axe and smashed the picture of the rat. There, trapped in the wires that supported the picture, was his beloved rat, who had died of starvation. The dead rat turned his head to face the man and said, *(As if imitating a ghost)* "If you had not been satisfied with my picture you could have had me. You chicken-hearted bastard," and then disintegrated into dust.

LEOPOLD   *(Frightened)* A fairy tale.

ISIDORE   There is a moral to it, Leopold. Try to understand it.

LEOPOLD   The dead don't speak.

ISIDORE   Yes, they do. You'll see, you'll see. Understand the story, Leopold. You must relinquish what you want or you will never have it.

LEOPOLD   I understand one thing. There is something that moves you. There is something that makes you tender and loving, only one thing: nastiness . . . and meanness and abuse.

ISIDORE   Those are three things, Leopold.

LEOPOLD   They're all the same.

ISIDORE   It's our fate.

LEOPOLD   Not mine. . . . I love . . .

ISIDORE   You don't love. All you do is whine!

LEOPOLD   It's time you answered my question, Isidore.

ISIDORE   I answered it.

LEOPOLD   You told me to gore you.

ISIDORE   Yes, I did.

LEOPOLD   Is that the answer?

ISIDORE   That was my answer.

LEOPOLD   You stabbed me. I want my answer.

ISIDORE   There is a way, Leopold, but only one. You must find it yourself.

LEOPOLD   That's no answer. You wounded me.

ISIDORE   You tried to gore me. I had to defend myself.

LEOPOLD   You told me to gore you.

ISIDORE   That was part of the game.

LEOPOLD   Stinking bastard. Can you bear your own rottenness? You must atone for your wickedness sometime. You cannot go on without a purge. Do you ever pray? Do you beat your fist against your chest and ask for forgiveness? If not to redeem yourself, at least to be able to go on with your viciousness. You could not endure it without a purge. Do you spend your nights covering your ears to keep away the sound of my moans? Do you cry then? . . . Could it be that you do it out of stupidity, that you don't know the difference between right and wrong? Oh no. Let it be anything but that. Let it be malice. If you do it out of a decision to be harmful, I can convince you that it's best to be good. But if you don't know the difference between right and wrong, is there anything I can do? Maybe you must be vicious in spite of yourself. Maybe you have to do it . . . to protect me from something worse? . . . for my own good?

LEOPOLD *throws himself on his knees with his head on* ISIDORE*'s lap.*

Give me a sign, a smile, a look. Tell me you love me.

ISIDORE *pouts innocently.* HE *makes a circle with his arm and places his hand on* LEOPOLD*'s head. The lights fade.*

SCENE 3

ISIDORE *and* LEOPOLD *are in the same position.* ISIDORE *stretches himself and yawns.* HE *jerks his thighs slightly to make* LEOPOLD*'s head roll and fall to the floor.* ISIDORE *looks at* LEOPOLD *who is waking up and smiles.* ISIDORE *stands up, stretches again, and does a dance step.*

ISIDORE   Cheery-uppy, Leopold.

The following scene is to have a nightmarish quality. ISIDORE
and LEOPOLD *dance in a ritualistic manner.* ISIDORE *puts on one
of the two beetle masks, the one which is wingless, and gives the
other to* LEOPOLD. LEOPOLD *should behave like a sleep-walker.*

Beetles are versatile little animals. For great numbers, the end
of autumn does not mean the end of their lives. There are more
beetles by far than any other kind of insect. Over a quarter of
a million beetle species have been described. Beetles are in
constant conflict with man because there are few of the organic
commodities that man has learned to use that do not also interest some beetle. Some spend their life in the thick flesh of
century-plant leaves and when caught make an excellent salad,
tasting something like shrimp salad. Other notable varieties are:
The Clavicornia, the segments of whose torso are variable in
number and whose antennae are equipped with a more or less
*(*ISIDORE *does a bump and grind)* distinct club, the terminal
segments being broader than the others. The Hydrophilidae
*(*ISIDORE *places his arms in arabesque position)* Silphidae, Sta-
phylinidae, Nitidulidae *(Convulsing)* Histeridae, Coccinellidae,
Ebonychidae *(Holding his breasts)* Erotylidae, Languiridae, and
Dermestidae. The literature of beetles is enormous.

LEOPOLD   *(Crawling on the floor)* When things are in disorder and
I move, I feel like I'm crawling. As if with every movement I
have to drag along with me the things that are in disorder. As
if I had grown brooms on my sides that extend as far as the wall,
to sweep the junk . . . the dust.

LEOPOLD *picks up some of the cards, looks at* ISIDORE *and smiles
sadly.*

ISIDORE   They are for your own good. Ingrate. Don't you know?
Come, do me a pretty beetle.

LEOPOLD   Dirt, my dear sir, comes to us from everywhere. And it comes out from within us. It comes out through each pore. Then we wash it away, we flush it away, we drown it, we bury it, we incinerate it, and then we perfume ourselves. We put odors in our toilets, medicinal odors, terrible odors, but all these odors seem sweet next to our own. What I want, sir, is to live with that loathsome mess near me, not to flush it away. To live with it for all those who throw perfume on it. To be so dirty for those who want to be so clean. To do them that favor. I wanted to drop it in the pot and leave it there for days, and live with it.

ISIDORE   Sometimes you touch the realm of romance.

LEOPOLD   In the latter part of the afternoon I feel cold, I feel the stuff in my bowels. And I feel downcast. The open air is in my mind, but my eyes wander around this cave. I feel such pain for being here.

ISIDORE   The contrast between your poet's taste for languid amusement and my unconventional pageantry sends such fresh impetus throbbing through my veins.

LEOPOLD   I see a light in you. The only light. I see it through a tunnel lower than myself. Attempting to go through it and hoping to be invited, I crawl.

ISIDORE   Crawl then. Crawl then.

LEOPOLD *crawls.*

LEOPOLD   I liked to think I was an exception, of course, I pretended I was not one more snake. And to prove I was an exception, I tried to stand erect, and to stand erect I needed you to support me, and when you refused me I had to beg, and to beg I had to crawl, and snakes crawl, and I am a snake. When crawling tires me, I stand erect. It is to exhaustion and disillusion that I owe my dignity. Not to pride . . . Oh . . . I cannot make your eyes turn to me with love.

ISIDORE   Give me a pretty smile, pretty beetle.

LEOPOLD *opens his mouth wide.*

LEOPOLD   To make dirt come out through the mouth you have to close your holes very tight, and let the dirt rot inside. Then it will come out through any opening.

ISIDORE   The prophet, the prophet. Come and hear the dirty prophet.

LEOPOLD   *(Taking off his mask)* Oh, Isidore, you are my enemy.

ISIDORE   I am not your enemy.

LEOPOLD   Come here. Let me see you.

ISIDORE *moves near* LEOPOLD.

Take that mask off.

ISIDORE *takes the mask off.*

You *are* my enemy.

ISSIDORE   What makes you say that?

LEOPOLD   Your smell . . .

ISIDORE   How do I smell?

LEOPOLD   You stink.

ISIDORE   Not true. What you smell is your own stink. You are putrid.

LEOPOLD   I'm going to kill you.

ISIDORE   Don't, you're trying to scare me. You're trying to scare me
    so I'll be good to you.

LEOPOLD   No . . . I know nothing can make you change. No . . . If
    I were to frighten you you'd behave for a while, but then you
    would get to like it, and you'd want more and more of it.

ISIDORE   And you wouldn't do it just to please your old friend?

LEOPOLD   No, I wouldn't. I have already played too many of your
    games. I have become as corrupt as you intended me to be. But
    . . . no more.

ISIDORE   You can't stop now. It's too late.

LEOPOLD   I know. That's why I've decided to kill you.

ISIDORE   You have?

    LEOPOLD *goes to the shrine and gets the knife.* ISIDORE *hides
    behind a piece of furniture and begins to tremble.*

LEOPOLD   Get up, Isidore.

ISIDORE   No.

    LEOPOLD *lifts the knife and holds it up for a moment, then lowers
    it slowly.*

LEOPOLD   If I killed you what would I be?

ISIDORE   A murderer . . . that's what you'd be . . . a murderer. A dirty
    ratty murderer.

LEOPOLD   There will be no one to judge me.

ISIDORE   Yourself . . . you'll judge yourself. You'll die of guilt.

LEOPOLD   Guilt . . . ? Is that what it is?

ISIDORE   Yes. And then you'll be all alone. You don't know what it is to be alone. It's horribly . . . lonely.

LEOPOLD   I'm afraid of my own death. I see myself dead.

ISIDORE   You're not going to do it then?

LEOPOLD   You're disappointed.

ISIDORE   Yes, I thought I was going to have some thrills and suspense, never knowing when you would strike . . . having to sleep with one eye open. But as usual you are a party-pooper . . . You could never kill me, Leopold. Don't you see? You are just what I want you to be. You only know what I have taught you. And I haven't taught you how to kill.

LEOPOLD   You have offended me. If you died I still would be offended.

ISIDORE   I have offended you and you haven't challenged me to a duel? Challenge me to a duel immediately . . . What kind of a mouse are you . . . I have offended you. I am offending you right now. You mouse. *(Smack)* You mouse. *(Smack)* You misbegotten mouse. You misbegotten, lifeless mouse.

LEOPOLD   If I killed you the offense would not be undone. If you died, you would not be able to atone for it.

ISIDORE   Don't worry, there isn't a chance of that. I'll kill you and be done with you.

ISIDORE *puts the sword in* LEOPOLD *'s hand.*

LEOPOLD   If you killed me you would be convinced that you had the right to offend me.

ISIDORE   Beautiful, beautiful. Let's duel. You'll fight for your offended pride. I, for the right to offend you. Come on. Come on.

LEOPOLD   Please stop, Isidore.

ISIDORE   No, this is fun. It's fun. *En garde.*

LEOPOLD   *(Poking different objects with his sword)* What are these things . . . Leopold? Leopold? Are you Leopold? Are you . . . they don't strike back. You are Leopold.

ISIDORE   Too much reflection.

ISIDORE *pokes* LEOPOLD *with the sword.* LEOPOLD *shrinks back.*

LEOPOLD   Each time I hold back I die a little.

ISIDORE   That's why you stink, you're putrid with death. Cleanliness is close to godliness. *(Card)* I still have a lot to teach you.

LEOPOLD   *(Swaying)* I feel faint. If only I could find a spot to fix on and steady myself.

ISIDORE   *(Swaying and lurching)* Look at me. Let me be the spot. Look, everything is moving. But I am steady as a rock.

LEOPOLD   Come here, Isidore. Open your arms.

ISIDORE *obeys.* LEOPOLD *lifts the sword slowly, points it to* ISIDORE*'s heart, and pushes it into his body.* ISIDORE *falls to the floor.*

ISIDORE   How could you do this?

LEOPOLD *holds* ISIDORE *in his arms.* HE *doesn't answer.*

Say you're sorry and my wound will heal.

LEOPOLD   I know.

ISIDORE   Say you're sorry.

LEOPOLD   If I do you'll curse me.

ISIDORE   I beg you, Leopold, I'm dying.

LEOPOLD   Die, Isidore . . . I understand now . . . You made it clear
enough . . .

ISIDORE *dies.*

It is done. All the thought and preparation did not help me do
it. It is done. And I don't know what made me do it. The
moment came. The only moment when it could be done. It
possessed me and I let it take me.

*The stage darkens. The door opens. The sound of harps is heard
outside. There is a blue sky.* ISIDORE *appears among the clouds
dressed as an angel.* HE *carries stacks of cards.* HE *beckons*
LEOPOLD *to follow him.* LEOPOLD *picks up a few cards, then the
sword, then a few more cards.* ISIDORE *shakes his head, and
shows* LEOPOLD *the cards* HE *carries.* LEOPOLD *walks through the
door slowly, but with determination.* HE *is ready for the next
stage of their battle.*

THE SUCCESSFUL LIFE OF 3

To Susan Sontag

The Successful Life of 3 was first presented at the Firehouse Theatre in Minneapolis, in a production underwritten by the University of Minnesota's Office for Advanced Drama Research, on January 22, 1965. It was directed and designed by the author, with the following cast:

He   *Jeff Moses*
She   *Carrie Bartlett*
3   *Mel Semler*
Policemen and Bodyguards   *Don Young, Edd Ward, Mike Monson*

The Successful Life of 3 was subsequently presented by the Open Theatre at the Sheridan Square Playhouse in New York, for a series of performances beginning on March 15, 1965. This production was directed initially by Joseph Chaikin, and then re-directed by Richard Gilman, with the following cast:

He   *James Barbosa*
She   *Barbara Vann*
3   *Paul Boesing*
Policemen and Bodyguards   *Sydney Schubert Walter, Ron Faber, Rhea Gaisner*

HE, a handsome young man
SHE, a sexy young lady
3, a plump, middle-aged man
BODYGUARDS
POLICEMEN

*** following a character's name indicates:

For SHE, that SHE thinks with a stupid expression (the OTHERS watch her)

For HE, that HE looks disdainful (the OTHERS watch him)

And for 3, that 3 looks with intense curiosity (the OTHERS watch him)

Very deadpan.

SCENE 1

The Doctor's Office. 3 and HE sit. HE is combing his hair. 3 takes a shoe off and drops it. At the sound of the shoe, HE becomes motionless, his arms suspended in the air. 3 looks at HE and freezes for a moment.

3   What are you doing?

HE   Waiting.

3   What for?

HE   For the other shoe to drop.

3   Ah, and I was wondering what you were doing. If I hadn't asked, we would have stayed like that forever. You waiting and me

wondering . . . That's the kind of person I am. I ask . . . That's good, you know.

HE   Why?

3   ***

HE   Why?

3   It starts action.

HE   What action did you start?

3   We're talking.

HE   That's nothing. We could as well be waiting for the shoe to drop.

> HE *suspends his arms in the air again.* 3 *stares at* HE. THEY *remain motionless for a while.*

3   Sorry . . . I'm going to do my sewing.

HE   First take the other shoe off. Get it over with.

3   *(Taking off his shoe)* I wasn't going to take it off. *(3 takes needle and thread and sews a button on his shirt)* You see? If I do it now I don't have to do it later.

HE   What?

3   The sewing.

HE   And what are you going to do later?

3   *** *(Puts the needle and thread away)* Look, there are advantages to being optimistic.

HE   Sure.

3   What are they?

HE   You tell me.

3   Well, it makes one feel happier.

HE   You don't look happy to me.

3   Oh, no?

HE   No.

3   Well, things are not what they appear to the eye.

HE   They aren't?

3   Are they?

HE   Sometimes . . . sometimes they are just what they appear to the eye . . . Don't generalize.

3   Why?

HE   Because there are always exceptions. There's always one that isn't like the others.

3   If it's just one, it can be thrown in with the rest. It doesn't matter.

HE   It matters.

3   Perhaps you can exclude it in your mind. Without mentioning it.

HE   You have to mention it . . . You're splitting hairs anyway.

3   I like splitting hairs.

HE   Well, do it when I'm not around.

3   I was just joking.

HE   *(Correcting him)* Being facetious.

3   *(Taking an apple from his pocket)* Want an apple?

HE   No.

3   An apple a day keeps the doctor away.

HE   I knew you were going to say that.

> SHE *enters wearing a nurse's uniform.*

Miss, you're a fine dish.

SHE   Thanks. *(SHE exits and re-enters)*

HE   Miss, I would like to bounce on you.

SHE   Thank you. *(To 3)* Come in please.

> 3 *and* SHE *exit.* SHE *re-enters.*

HE   Miss, I would like to bang you.

SHE   Your friend just did.

HE   Well, I'm next.

SHE   I only do it once a day.

HE   I get you all worked up and you do it with him instead?

SHE   ***

HE   I'm handsome and sexy and I get you all worked up, and you go and do it with him? Answer now.

SHE   What?

HE   Is that natural?

SHE   I don't know.

    3 *enters.*

HE   A moment ago I was thinking of marrying you.

SHE   You just saw me for the first time.

3   He figured he'd see you a few more times if he married you.

HE   Don't speak for me after you ruined everything . . . Let me try again. Miss, would you go to the movies with me after work?

SHE   Okay, I like the movies.

HE   Everybody likes the movies.

SHE   I never liked them until a few months ago.

HE   What made you like them then?

SHE   I saw a movie with the Lane sisters.

HE   You like them?

SHE   Yes, they're all right.

HE   What do they do?

SHE   Stupid things.

HE   Like what?

SHE   They cry and laugh.

HE   That doesn't sound so great.

SHE   I like it. It's all right if you like sisters.

3   I like movies about marriage, divorce and remarriage.

SHE   I like sisters.

HE   I don't have any particular preference. I just like good movies
. . . with action and a lot of killing.

SHE   I couldn't go to the movies if I didn't have a preference.

3   Neither could I.

    3 takes SHE *by the hand and exits.* SHE *re-enters.*

HE   Did you make it with him again?

SHE   Yes.

HE   How long are you going to keep this up?

SHE   I don't know.

    3 re-enters.

HE   Listen, I was even thinking of marrying you.

SHE   You'd have to give me a ring for that. Two rings. An engagement ring and a wedding band.

3   I'll give the bride away.

HE   From the looks of it you're not leaving anything to give away.

3   And I'm not through yet.

HE   I didn't say you were.

3   You didn't say I was but you sure wish I were.

SHE   Me too.

HE   I never wish.

SHE   In my profession you have to wish.

3   For what?

SHE   ***

HE   I don't have a profession.

SHE   How are you going to support me?

HE   I'll find a way.

3   He sure does have to support you. Doesn't he?

SHE   Yeah, my parents pay for the wedding and he supports me.

3   I'll pay for the wedding.

HE   He doesn't have any money. Get your parents to pay for the wedding.

SHE   Weddings are a pain in the neck.

3   Why do you want one then?

SHE   ***

HE   Don't you see she doesn't know?

3   Yes, I see.

SHE   The Andrews sisters are all married.

HE   Do you like brothers too?

SHE   Not so much.

HE   Did you see *The Corsican Brothers?*

SHE   That's not brothers. That's just Douglas Fairbanks playing twins. It's not the same.

HE   What brothers do you like?

SHE   I don't know any.

HE   How do you know you like them?

SHE   ***

3   She didn't say she liked them.

HE   Didn't you say you like them?

SHE   No, I said, "Not so much" . . . I don't think I'm going to marry you.

3   Why?

HE   I can ask my own questions, if you please. *(To* SHE*)* Why?

SHE   You're too picky.

HE   That's all right. Are we going to the movies or not?

SHE Sure.

3 If you find a sister movie.

SHE That's all right. I'll try another kind.

3 Let's go in for a quickie before you leave.

>   *3 and* SHE *exit,* SHE *re-enters wearing a hat.*

HE Ready?

SHE Yes.

HE Hey, didn't you say you only do it once a day?

SHE Yes.

HE How come you did it with him three times already?

SHE ***

HE You're not a liar, are you?

SHE No.

HE You better not be, because I can't stand liars.

>   *3 re-enters.* HE *and* SHE *exit.*

3 Wait for me. *(3 exits)*

SCENE 2

> *The Movies. The lights go down and flicker.* HE, 3 *and* SHE *enter.*
> THEY *sit—3 in the middle,* SHE *and* HE *at his sides.*

HE   Hey, what do you mean by sitting next to her? Change with me. She's my date.

3   I can't feel her up from there.

HE   You don't have to feel her up.

3 *and* HE *change seats.*

3   How about some popcorn?

SHE   I'll go.

3   Don't go. Let him go.

HE   You go.

3   I can't.

HE *exits.* 3 *moves next to* SHE. HE *re-enters.*

HE   Move back to your seat.

3   I already moved once. I'm not moving twice. Let's have some popcorn.

HE *offers popcorn to* 3.

I'll hold it because I'm in the middle.

3 *tries to hold the bag, eat popcorn, and feel* SHE *up.*

You hold the bag. I can't feel her up and eat at the same time if I hold the bag.

HE *takes the bag.*

HE   At least wait till the feature starts.

SCENE 3

The Porch. Ten years later. HE *dozes.* SHE *peels potatoes.* 3 *sews.*

SHE   I'm going to divorce him.

3   Give him another chance.

SHE   Him?

3   He's not bad.

SHE   Yes, he is.

3   There are worse.

SHE   No, there aren't.

3   Wouldn't it be worse if you were married to me?

SHE   What difference would it make?

3   It would make a difference.

SHE   No, it wouldn't.

3   Yes, it would.

SHE   What difference?

3   ***

SHE   What difference?

3   I'll ask him

    3 *shakes* HE.

Hey, would it make any difference if she was married to me instead of you?

HE   Yeah.

3   What difference?

HE   Ask her. She ought to know.

3   She doesn't know.

HE   She never knows anything.

3   Actually, this time she knows. She said it wouldn't make any difference.

HE   She's probably right, because she usually doesn't know anything.

SHE   I'm going to divorce him whether I'm right or wrong.

3   Marry a worse one for a while . . . then remarry him and you'll be happier.

HE   That would be like wearing tight shoes so it feels better when you take them off.

3   That's the idea. Do it.

SHE   You can't do that.

3   Why not?

SHE   I don't know.

3   (To HE) Do you know why you can't wear tight shoes so it feels better when you take them off?

HE   No.

SHE   But isn't it true that you're not supposed to?

HE   Yeah.

SHE   I knew it.

3   Well, you'd be happier if you did it.

SHE   You're not supposed to.

HE   *(To 3)* Get off that chair. I want to put my feet up.

   3 *moves to another chair.*

3   Rivalry.

SHE   What?

3   Rivalry.

SHE   ***

3   Masculine rivalry.

SHE   ***

3   Masculine rivalry. *(3 points to* HE *and to himself)*

SHE   Who ever heard of such a thing.

3   What?

SHE   What you said.

3   Rivalry?

SHE   Yeah.

3   You haven't heard of it?

SHE   No.

3   I bet you he has. *(To* HE*)* Have you heard of rivalry?

HE   Sure.

3   See?

SHE   I mean the other.

3   Masculine?

SHE   Both, both together.

3   *(To* HE*)* Have you heard of masculine rivalry?

HE   Yeah.

SHE   So he has.

>   *3 looks* SHE *over.*

3   I don't desire you any more.

SHE   Thank God.

3   Don't thank God. Thank me.

SHE   Stop picking on me.

HE   Are you picking on her again?

3   I can't help it.

HE   Stop picking on her.

3   Masculine rivalry.

HE   What are you talking about? There's no comparison. I'm sexy
and you're slimy.

SHE   That's the only thing I like about him.

HE   You like *that?*

SHE   It's all right . . . But I'm tired of having children.

HE   That's not true. You told me you like children.

SHE   Not that many.

3   How many are there?

SHE   I don't know.

3   How do you know there are too many?

SHE   ***

3   I'll go count them. *(3 exits)*

HE   Listen, you can't one day say you like babies and the next day
say you don't.

SHE   Why not?

HE   You have to make up your mind.

SHE   *** (SHE *doesn't answer)*

HE   Well?

SHE   I can't stand the twins.

HE   Why not?

SHE   They look too much alike.

HE   Twins always do.

SHE   I didn't say they didn't.

HE   You didn't say they did either.

SHE   No, all I said was that I didn't like them.

HE   Why?

SHE   I don't see why they have to dress alike.

HE   Twins always do.

SHE   I didn't say they didn't.

HE   Bring the food out.

SHE   There's no food.

HE   How come?

SHE   You know how come.

HE   No, I don't.

SHE   You're supposed to provide for me, but you don't.

HE   Don't I get you all the potatoes?

SHE   I'm going. I can't stand peeling potatoes all the time.

SHE *exits. 3 enters.*

HE   She left.

3   Oh.

HE   That's all right. I never want what I don't have.

3   I missed it.

HE   What?

3   Her leaving. I've been waiting around to see her leave, and now she does it when I'm not looking. How did she go?

HE   ***

SCENE 4

The porch. Three years later. HE *peels potatoes,* 3 *sews.*

3   I'm going into business. I can't stand this home life any longer.

HE   You wouldn't be any good at it.

3   I might as well try it.

HE   You would just lose all your money.

3   I don't have any money.

HE   How're you going to go into business?

3   I'll put a bid on some nylon rope, go south, convince the fishermen to use nylon instead of whatever they use, and take them for all they've got.

HE   They probably use nylon.

3   Then I'll sell it to them cheap and still make a fortune.

HE   It wouldn't work.

3   No? . . . Well, I can make a sandwich with peanut butter and Ritz crackers, dip it in chocolate, call it Tootsie Tootsie, and sell it.

HE   You're better off with the nylon rope.

3   I thought so too. I'll go try it.

HE   Okay.

3   Good-bye. Give my love to Ruth if you see her. Have you seen her?

HE   Yes, she's happily married.

3   Who to?

HE   I don't know.

3   Well, if you see her, tell her I would still like a roll in the hay with her, even if she's getting old and decrepit.

HE   Okay, I'll tell her.

3   Good-bye. You do think it will work?

HE   Sure.

3   Good-bye then. *(3 exits)*

HE   Just said that to get rid of him.

3   *(Re-enters, wearing top hat and furs)* It worked.

HE   Don't tell me it worked.

3   *(Respectfully)* Oh, sorry.

HE   What do you mean it worked?

3   I put a bid on some nylon rope, went south, convinced them fishermen to use nylon instead of whatever they were using, and took them for all they had. D'you know rope is sold by the weight, not the measure?

HE   Don't get smart with me, Arthur. I'm very annoyed. I have all the brains and the looks and it's you who goes south with your squeaky voice and sweaty hands and makes all the money.

3   And I'm not finished yet. I'm going to make that peanut butter sandwich and make another mint.

HE   You're making me sick.

3   Don't get sick yet. I'm just starting. You think Ruth likes money?

HE   Sure.

3   Perhaps she'll come live with us for the money. It'll be good for the children.

HE   I'm the husband and the father. I'll make my own decisions.

3   Yeah, but I do all the screwing and make all the money.

HE   Don't rub it in.

3   Sorry.

HE   You may make all the money and all that, but you have no manners.

3   Teach me manners.

HE *puts on the top hat and furs.* SHE *enters.*

SHE   Okay, I came back.

HE   Because of the money.

SHE   I like money.

HE   Everybody likes money. You say it as if it was something special.

SHE   It is special. I like money very much.

3   More than sisters?

SHE   ***

HE   Never mind.

3   I have a present for you.

3 *gives* SHE *three men's hats.*

SHE   These are men's hats. What's the matter with you?

3   Nothing.

HE   He doesn't know his ass from his elbow.

3   I do. *(3 points to his buttocks and his elbow)* I only didn't know what kind of hat to buy.

SHE   Where's the money?

3   In the bank.

SHE   Oh, damn it. I came for the money and you put it away.

HE   You didn't come for that. You didn't come for that. You came for me and for the children.

SHE   You said I came for the money.

HE   I was just accusing you.

SHE   And what was I supposed to say?

HE   "I didn't. I didn't. I came for you and the children." Defend yourself.

SHE   Well, I didn't.

HE   I don't have to stay here while you come back for his money. I'm sexy and bright and you're a bunch of morons. I'm leaving.

3 *puts his arm around* SHE.

You don't have to jump on her the moment I turn my back.

3 *lets go of* SHE.

SHE   I'm glad he caught you.

HE   You can do what you want. I'm leaving. Good-bye. *(*HE *exits)*

SHE   What are we going to do without him?

3   Wait for him.

SCENE 5

The Store. Three years later. HE *is standing.* 3 *steals a pipe.*

HE   Arthur!

3   What are you doing here?

HE   I'm a store detective.

3   How long have you been a store detective?

HE   Since I left the house.

3   Is the pay good?

HE   Not for the risk you take.

3   What risk?

HE   You might get hit or knifed.

3   Who would do that?

HE   The thief. You see, I grab him like this. I identify myself and I tell him to go with me to the office. Then he either becomes frightened and comes along quietly, or becomes violent and attacks me.

(3 punches HE *and runs)*

SCENE 6

The Porch. A few minutes later. SHE *peels potatoes.* 3 *enters smoking the pipe.*

3   I just saw him. He's a detective.

SHE I don't like detectives.

3 Why?

SHE I can't understand them.

3 Why not?

SHE They talk too fast.

3 He's a store detective. They don't talk fast.

SHE A store detective is not a real detective.

3 Someone stole something though.

SHE Did he figure out who did it?

3 I don't know. I hit him and ran.

SHE You didn't run so fast. You're late for dinner. . . . Did you figure
out who did it?

3 Yeah, I did it.

SHE What did you do?

3 *(Showing her the pipe)* Stole it.

HE *enters.*

HE Why did you hit me?

SHE Is that a way to come in after you've been gone for three years?
Can't you say hello?

HE I don't feel like saying hello.

SHE   You could at least pretend.

HE   Why did you hit me?

3   Because I had to.

HE   Why?

3   Because I'm the thief and you're the detective.

HE   What did you steal?

3   Guess.

HE   I give up.

3   The pipe.

HE   Now I have to take you in.

3   You have to identify yourself.

HE   Don't be silly. You know me. Come on.

3   Good-bye, Ruth.

SHE   Good-bye.

SCENE 7

The Porch. Three days later. SHE *and* HE *are sitting.*

SHE   How come you came back now?

HE   Because he's away. . . . Masculine rivalry.

SHE   That's what he always says.

HE   So what. It's true.

SHE   How come he was stealing?

HE   He didn't know he could take the money out of the bank.

SHE   Can he?

HE   Yeah.

3   *(Enters wearing a prisoner's uniform)* I organized a revolt and got out.

HE   Can't you stay put in one place?

3   Can't I?

HE   No, you're always jumping from place to place.

3   I'll stay put now. Ruth, even if you're getting old and decrepit, I still want you. Jail makes a man want a woman.

HE   You disgust me. You spend three days in jail and you don't learn anything.

3   I did so. I organized the prisoners and now I'm the head of the mob. If you want I'll make you my bodyguard.

HE   You call that a body?

3   I know. I have to do some exercise. But in the meantime it's all right to call it a body.

HE   It is not all right with me. I'm leaving.

SHE He's always leaving.

3 Like Shane . . . Stay and have some fun. The guys are coming presently.

HE What kind of idiot are you that says presently?

3 No idiot. I'm the Alec Guinness type gangster.

HE God damn it. I'm getting fed up. You have no style, no looks, you act like an old housewife, and it's you who gets to go to jail and become the head of the mob.

SHE Let's eat.

HE Okay, but if you want me to be your bodyguard, you have to give me a good salary . . . No. I don't care if you get slugged. Good-bye. (HE *exits*)

3 You be my bodyguard, Ruth.

SHE Okay, but I don't move from this chair.

3 You have to move. You have to keep an eye on me.

SHE Skip it. Who wants to look at you all the time.

3 Okay. Don't be my bodyguard. I'll get the guys to look after me.

SCENE 8

The Porch. Six months later. 3 *and* SHE *sit.* 3 *is armed to the teeth.* BODYGUARDS *surround him.*

3 I have a sweet streak in me.

SHE   Where?

3   ***

SHE   What did you say?

3   I have a sweet streak in me.

SHE   Me too.

3   I'm tired of the life of crime.

SHE   Why don't you stop stealing?

3   I like stealing.

SHE   I thought you said you were tired of crime.

3   Yes, but not of stealing.

SHE   You're not supposed to steal.

3   Says who?

SHE   ***

3   You don't know anything. I'm going to steal from the rich and give to the poor.

SHE   I came back for the money and you're going to give it to the poor? I'm leaving.

3   Where are you going?

SHE   I'll go find a Joan Fontaine movie.

3   What good would that do you?

SHE   She's Olivia de Havilland's sister.

3   No, she's not.

SHE   Yes, she is.

3   They don't look alike.

SHE   The Lane sisters don't look alike either.

3   No, but they act like sisters.

SHE   ***

    3 *exits.* SHE *stands puzzled.*

SCENE 9

The Store. A few minutes later. HE *is standing.* 3 *walks by surrounded by* BODYGUARDS.

HE   Come with me to the office. You penny-pinching sonofabitch hoodlum. I finally caught you.

3   What for? I just came to get a Zorro costume. *(3 puts on a Zorro costume)*

HE   You look like an idiot, like you always did. Did you steal it?

3   I bought it.

HE   Show me the sales slip.

3   I lost it.

HE   You stole it. *(To the* BODYGUARDS*)* Did he steal it?

BODYGUARDS Yeah.

HE Come with me.

3 Don't be silly. If I'm Zorro and the store is rich, I have to steal from it. Now I have to give something to the poor. Here's a penny.

HE I'm turning you in anyway. I'll get fired if I don't catch someone soon. . . . I haven't caught anyone since the last time I caught you. Get moving.

3 No, I won't. I have better things to do, like ride around the pampas with my mask on. Come with me and you can ride too.

HE What kind of idiot d'you think I am. You'll make me do all the riding and cut all the Z's and you'll get all the credit. You do your own dirty work.

3 No, I won't . . . I'm getting too old to ride around like an idiot.

HE You used to do your own dirty work.

3 Yeah. But now I'm rich and lazy. *(To a* BODYGUARD*)* Can you ride?

BODYGUARD *shakes his head.*

Can you ride?

BODYGUARD *shakes his head.*

Can you ride?

BODYGUARD *shakes his head.*

Get out of my way. I don't need you any more. *(To* HE*)* Can Ruth ride?

HE No, she can't do anything.

3 That's all right. I'll go to some rodeo and get myself a double. *(3 exits)*

SCENE 10

The Porch. Three days later. HE *sits.* 3 *enters panting.*

3 Hide me.

HE What from?

3 I'm being followed.

HE What did you do?

3 I got tired of stealing from the rich and giving to the poor and started stealing from the rich and the poor. Hide me.

HE I won't hide you. I don't care if they catch you.

3 Hide my *antifaz* then.

HE What's that?

3 My mask. Do you know that Zorro means fox in Spanish?

HE Never mind. I don't care if Zorro means fox. I can't hide your *antifaz*. I'll lose my job if I get caught with stolen goods.

3 I thought they were going to fire you.

HE I caught a girl who didn't do anything and they let me stay.

3 That's not nice. Where's Ruth?

HE   She went to see Joan Fontaine and never came back.

3   Did she take any money with her?

HE   She doesn't need any money. She married the guy who owns the movie.

3   How're the children?

HE   They're all right. They're always playing doctor.

3   Are they sick?

HE   No, they just play doctor.

The POLICEMEN *enter and grab* 3.

3   Where're you taking me?

POLICEMEN   To the scaffold.

3   Oh! Merciful God.

The POLICEMEN *take* 3 *away.* 3 *re-enters, carrying a bouquet.*

HE   I thought they were going to hang you.

3   I got out of it. Here's Ruth. She must have broken up with that movie man.

SHE *enters.* 3 *gives her the flowers.*

SHE   How did you know I was coming?

3   I didn't.

HE   How did you get out?

3   I told them you did it.

HE   I'll lose my job at the store.

3   Don't let that worry you. You won't need a job any more. They're coming to get you any minute. *(To* SHE*)* What made you come back?

SHE   I'm old and tired and I've had too many men. I'm just going to sit here and rest for the rest of my life.

3   Oh no you won't. You have to work for your keep. Scrub the floor.

HE   I'm going to the store. I can't stand seeing my wife scrubbing floors.

SHE   Don't go. I'm not going to scrub no floors. You've become a mean old sonofabitch, Arthur.

3   I was always mean. I just didn't know it.

SHE   You're not supposed to be mean.

3   Why not?

SHE   ***

HE   She's right. You're not supposed to be mean.

SHE   I knew it.

3   Well, perhaps I just have a mean streak in me.

SHE   Yeah, like the Grand Canyon.

HE   The Grand Canyon is not a streak.

SHE   What is it?

3   It's a ditch.

SHE   Same thing.

3   Well, here are the cops anyway. They're coming to get you.

HE   You're disgusting. You go around being a sonofabitch and then you pin it on me. What am I going to do now?

3   ***

SHE   ***

HE   You're a bunch of morons.

> The POLICEMEN enter. THEY grab 3.

3   Where are you taking me?

POLICEMEN   To the scaffold.

3   I just came from there.

> The POLICEMEN take 3 away.

SHE   Are you going to miss him?

HE   No, he's a sonofabitch—are you?

SHE   What?

HE   Going to miss him?

SHE   ***

3 *enters with a bouquet of flowers and gives them to* SHE.

HE   How come you always come back with flowers?

3   They have them there.

SHE   What for?

3   For the grave.

HE   Did you steal them?

3   No, they give them to you.

SHE   They go bad if they don't use them.

HE   How did you get away this time?

3   They caught the real Zorro.

SHE   I thought you were the real Zorro.

3   No, I'm too young.

HE   Bring in the food, Ruth.

SHE   What food?

3   I have some Tootsie Tootsies.

> THEY *eat Tootsie Tootsies. A* POLICEMAN *enters.* 3 *shoots him dead.*

I'm not armed to the teeth for nothing.

> THEY *freeze for a moment. Then* THEY *sing the "Song to Ignorance."*

ALL

> Let me be wrong.
> But also not know it.
> Be wrong,
> Be wrong,
> And, oh, not to know it.
> Oh! Let me be wrong.

3

> One day while walking
> Down the street,
> I found a petunia
> And took it.
> I took it.
> Oh! Let me be wrong.

ALL

> Let me be wrong.
> But also not know it.
> Be wrong,
> Be wrong,
> And, oh, not to know it.
> Oh! Let me be wrong.

SHE

> I went from here

HE

> To where?

SHE

> I don't know where.
> I called a parasol an umbrella.

Yes, an umbrella.
Oh, let me be wrong.
I don't care.

ALL

Let me be wrong.
But also not know it.
Be wrong,
Be wrong,
And, oh, not to know it.
Oh! Let me be wrong.

HE

I sprechen sie dutch very well
I said to Herr Auber:
Herr Auber, I sprechen sie
Dutch very well, Herr Auber.
Oh! Let me be wrong.

ALL

Let me be wrong.
But also not know it.
Be wrong,
Be wrong,
And, oh, not to know it.
Oh! Let me be wrong.
Oh! Let me be wrong.
Oh! Let me be wrong.
I want to be wrong!

THEY *repeat the song and walk down the aisles selling Tootsie Tootsies.*

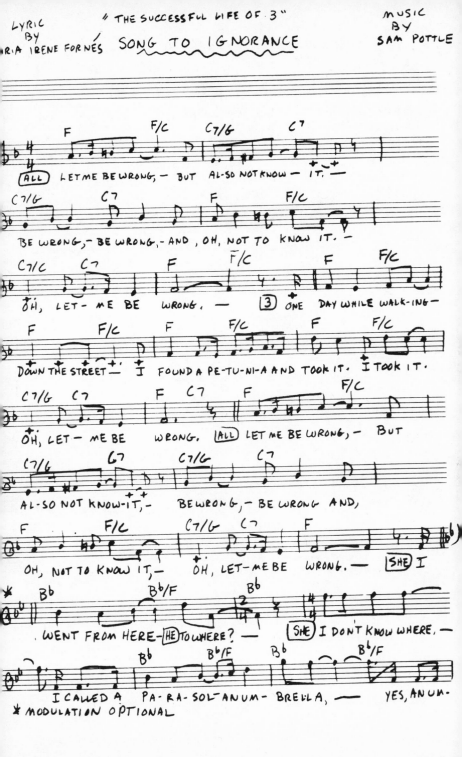

OH, LET — ME BE WRONG. — OH, LET- ME BE WRONG.—

OH, LET- ME BE WRONG, BE WRONG, —

I WANT— TO BE WRONG.

D.S. (f.) FOR PLAYOFF

PROMENADE

Promenade was first performed by the Judson Poets Theatre at Judson Memorial Church in New York on April 9, 1965. The music was composed by Al Carmines, and the play was directed by Lawrence Kornfeld, with musical direction by the composer, sets by Malcolm Spooner, costumes by the author and Ellen Levene, lighting by Kathy Lewis, and the following cast:

105	*David Vaughn*
106	*George Bartenieff*
Jailer	*Michael Elias*
Miss I	*Gretel Cummings*
Miss O	*Crystal Field*
Miss U	*Joan Fairlee*
Mr. R	*John Toland*
Mr. S	*Christopher Jones*
Mr. T	*Christopher Ross*
Servant	*Sheila Roy*
Miss Cake	*Florence Tarlow*
Waiter	*Howard Roy*
Chinaman	*Frank Emerson*
Warden	*William Pardue*
Mother	*Jerri Banks*

An expanded version of *Promenade* was the inaugural production at the Promenade Theatre, New York, opening June 4, 1969. This production was also directed by Mr. Kornfeld, with scenery by Rouben Ter-Arutunian, costumes by Willa Kim, lighting by Jules Fisher, orchestrations by Eddie Sauter, musical direction by the composer, orchestra conducted by Susan Romann, and the following cast:

105   *Ty McConnell*
106   *Gilbert Price*
Jailer   *Pierre Epstein*
Servant   *Madeline Kahn*
Miss I   *Margot Albert*
Miss O   *Carrie Wilson*
Miss U   *Alice Playten*
Mr. R   *Marc Allen III*
Mr. S   *Glenn Kezer*
Mr. T   *Michael Davis*
Waiter   *Edmund Gaynes*
Rosita (Miss Cake)   *Florence Tarlow*
Dishwasher   *Art Ostrin*
Mayor   *George S. Irving*
Mother   *Shannon Bolin*

The version of *Promenade* published here has been slightly revised from the text of the 1969 production. Scenes performed in that production and subsequently omitted may be found in an Appendix following the text of the play.

Photograph:
The Warden and
Miss Cake, Judson Poets
Theatre production

CHARACTERS

105
106
JAILER
SERVANT
MISS I
MISS O
MISS U
MR. R
MR. S
MR. T
MISS CAKE
WAITER
DISHWASHER
DRIVER
INJURED MAN
MOTHER
SOLDIER I
SOLDIER II

The roles of WAITER, DRIVER and SOLDIER I are to be played by one actor. So are the roles of DISHWASHER, INJURED MAN and SOLDIER II.

ACT I / SCENE 1

The Cell. 105 *and* 106 *dig and sing. The* JAILER *enters.* HE *is out of breath.* HE *sits and dries his forehead.*

105 and 106

Dig, dig, dig
A hole to be free.
Dig a hole, dig a hole,
A hole to be free.

JAILER   It's been a hard day.

105 and 106

   Dig, dig, dig.

JAILER   Screwing all day.

105 and 106

   A hole to be free.

JAILER   Can't let the ladies visit the inmates unless they pay dues.

105 and 106

   Dig a hole, dig a hole,
   A hole to be free.

JAILER   Oh, it's been a hard day. 34's wife, 48's daughter, 108's widow.

105 and 106

   Fly the coop.
   Break the wall.
   See the sun.

JAILER   Well, better get back to the ladies. Just came up for some air. . . . What are you two doing there?

105 and 106

   Dig a hole, dig a hole,
   A hole to be free.

JAILER   Hm. You look like you're digging. Well, I better get back to the widow before she finds out her old man's dead.

105 and 106

> Unacquainted with evil we are.
> This shelter protects us from wrong.
> To discover the appearance of sin
> We must go where the dog takes a leak.

JAILER   So long, boys . . . By the way, if you want to get visitors just let me know. *(The* JAILER *laughs loudly as* HE *walks away)* I can arrange it for you.

105 and 106

> The hole is dug.
> Here we go.

> *105 and 106 disappear through the hole.*

SCENE 2

The Banquet. There are LADIES *and* GENTLEMEN *in evening clothes around the table. The* SERVANT *sweeps. The* WAITER *serves the* GUESTS. *105 and 106 enter.* THEY *put on top hats and tails.* THEY *sit at the table and eat.*

MR. R   Speech . . . speech . . .

MR. S   Let's play croquet. . . .

MR. R   Speeches and music . . .

MR. T   Let's call Mr. Lipschitz. . . .

MR. S   No speeches. . . . No speeches. . . .

MR. R   Let's have a song. . . .

105 *and* 106 *clear their throats.*

MISS O   Mr. T, was that you I saw on the corner of Fifth and Tenth?

MR. T   Perhaps.

MISS O   With Mrs. Schumann and her newly clipped poodle?

MR. T   Oh, no, it wasn't I. Friday night I was out of town.

MISS O   Ah! And how did you know it was Friday night I saw you on the corner of Fifth?

THEY *all laugh.*

MR. T   Well, I must confess. The lady loves me.

THEY *all laugh.*

MISS U   She shows good taste.

MR. R   Then, introduce us. She'll surely fall for me.

The LADIES *giggle.*

(Mr. R writes in a notebook) Mrs. Schumann . . . lady of taste. . . . Bring dog biscuit. *(To* MR. T*)* What is her address?

MR. T   Tch-Tch.

MISS I   Oh, Mr. R, what perspicacity.

MISS O   Are you sure that's what you mean?

MISS I *looks a little embarrassed.*

MR. S   Let's have a song.

105 and 106 stand and get ready to sing.

MISS O   And who are these? Dear me.

105 and 106 realize THEY *have been indiscreet.* THEY *sit back at the table and pretend not to hear the* OTHERS.

MISS I   They must be friends of Mr. S.

MISS U   My dear. You go right to the point. . . .

MISS I   Mr. S does frequent rather unearthly places, doesn't he?

MR. T   What do you mean?

MISS I   I mean the lower depths.

MR. T   Oh, yes.

MR. S   If I am sometimes in the company of this and that, my dear, it's only because I like to study life. . . . I am what you might call a student of life. . . . This . . . and that.

MISS U   Oh, how incredibly personal you are, Mr. S. Have I not always said you have the artist in you?

MR. S   I am neither more than I seem to be, nor more than I am, and no less, also.

SERVANT   *(Mimicking in a low voice)* And no less . . . also.

MR. R   Miss I . . .

MISS I   Yes?

MR. R   Last Saturday I waited for a certain lady who never arrived.

MISS I   You did?

MR. R   Yes.

MISS I   Oh, she couldn't come. She spent all afternoon walking up and down a certain street where a gentleman *(Referring to* MR. T*)* who shall remain nameless lives. She was hoping to have an accidental meeting . . . a sort of unexpected encounter with him. But he never left his house . . . nor did he enter it.

> MISS O *and* MISS U *giggle. The* SERVANT *is bored by the* LADIES' *and* GENTLEMEN'*s repartee. Through the following speeches* SHE *pantomimes their gestures.*

MR. T   He didn't, Madam . . . he didn't. He saw the lady from his window and she did indeed walk up and down his street. But he couldn't receive her . . . his heart was torn. You see, he received a letter from the one he loves *(Referring to* MISS U*)* telling him his love was unrequited. He spent all afternoon sitting by his window plucking petals from flowers, and the answer always was . . . she loves me not.

MISS O   And who is this he speaks of?

MISS U   She is not free to love. Her heart belongs to he *(Referring to* MR. S*)* whose glance drives her to a frenzy, and whose mere presence brings color to her cheeks.

MR. S   The man who puts you in such a state has eyes only for O. Oh, Miss O.

MISS I   Oh! What tension! A name has been mentioned.

MISS U   And what have you to say to that, O?

MISS O   I regret I cannot speak since Mr. S has mentioned me by name. But do you wonder why O shuns you when you are so indiscreet? *(Taking a step toward R)* And besides, she loves R.

R *takes a step toward* I.
I *takes a step toward* T.
T *takes a step toward* U.
U *takes a step toward* S.
S *takes a step toward* O.
O *takes a step toward* R.

MISS U

You were there when I was not.
I was there when you were not.
Don't love me, sweetheart,
Or I might stop loving you.

Unrequited love,
Unrequited love.

MISS O

Passionate lips are sweet.
But oh, how much sweeter
Are lips that refuse.
Don't love me, sweetheart,
Or I might stop loving you.

MISS I

Inviting lips,
Alluring lips
Which shape the word no
No no no no no no.
Don't love me, sweetheart,
Or I might stop loving you.

MR. R

You know nothing of life,
You know nothing of love

Till you have tasted
Of unrequited love.
Don't love me, sweetheart,
Or I might stop loving you.

ALL

Unrequited love,
Unrequited love.
There is no love
Like unrequited love.

MISS I   Oh! We sang that well.

MR. R   He who scrubs the pot finds it most shiny.

MR. S   *(To* MR. R*)* And he who soils it, turns up his nose. Mr. R, you were flat.

MISS I   Touché!

MISS U   What a marvelous mind.

MR. S   Just frank.

SERVANT   *(Mimicking)* Just frank.

THEY *all look at the* SERVANT, *shocked.*

MISS I   Mr. S, it's up to you to think of a rejoinder.

MR. S   Dear me, I'm speechless. Wait! Listen to my answer. *(*HE *improvises the following:)*

My frankness, my dear,
My wit, my veneer,
Are something you should revere.

LADIES   A rhyme! A rhyme!

MR. S

Instead, you just think it queer.
Your unprosperous status
Produces a dubious,
Fallacious, and tedious
Outlook on life.

The SERVANT *makes a face at him.*

You do not know what we're about
We do not know what you're about
Or care to know.

The SERVANT *lowers her head.*

It's sad your career
Depends on our whim.
On with your work, my dear,
Or you'll get thin.
You see, even if you're here,
And we're also here,
You are not near.
Isn't that clear?

MISS U   Oh, Mr. S., how well you rhyme.

MR. S   Not difficult, dear. Just keep the ending of the word in mind
. . . it will come.

MISS U   *Incendo, incendis, incendit, incendimos, incenditis, incen-
dunt.*

MR. S   No, dear, the ending, not the beginning.

MISS U   But Mr. S, how can one tell how a word will end?

MR. S   Foresight.

The WAITER *brings in a giant cake to the accompaniment of musical fanfare. The* DISHWASHER *follows.*

MR. T   Oh look! Look! Look! The cake is here.

MR. S   Oh look! Look! Look! It's time for dessert.

LADIES

> Don't eat it,
> Don't eat it.
> Wait until midnight.

GENTLEMEN

> Put it on the table,
> Put it on the table.

MISS U   Phooey. . . . It smells of garlic.

GENTLEMEN

> It's not to be eaten,
> It's not to be eaten.

MISS CAKE *steps out of the cake.* THEY *all applaud and cheer.*

LADIES

> Don't eat her,
> Don't eat her.
> Wait until midnight.

GENTLEMEN

> Put her on the table,
> Put her on the table.

LADIES

> She's not to be eaten,
> She's not to be eaten.

MISS I   What is she for?

DISHWASHER   To look at.

> *The* JAILER *'s head appears through the door.*

MR. S   And to touch.

MR. R   Only to touch.

DISHWASHER   And to look at.

MISS I   May the ladies touch, too?

MR. R   No, not the ladies, only the gentlemen.

MISS O   I want to be naked too.

MR. R

> Only one,
> Only one
> Naked lady.

MISS O   *(Taking off her dress)*

> Two . . . two. . . .
> I want to be naked too.

MR. R

> Only one,
> Only one
> Naked lady.
> All right,
> Two naked ladies.

MISS O

> Thank you,
> Thank you, sir.

GENTLEMEN

> Only two,
> Only two
> Naked ladies.

MISS I   *(Taking off her dress)*

> Three . . . three. . . .
> I want to be naked too.

GENTLEMEN

> Only two,
> Only two
> Naked ladies.
> All right,
> Three naked ladies.

MISS I

> Thank you,
> Thank you, sir.

GENTLEMEN

> Only three,
> Only three
> Naked ladies.

MISS U *(Taking off her dress)*

> Four . . . four. . . .
> I want to be naked too.

GENTLEMEN

> Only three,
> Only three
> Naked ladies.
> All right,
> Four naked ladies.

MISS U

> Thank you,
> Thank you, sir.

ALL

> Only four,
> Only four
> Naked ladies.
> Four . . . four . . .
> Four naked ladies.

LADIES

> Thank you,
> Thank you, sir.

MISS I *Mademoiselle, comment vous appelez-vous?*

MISS CAKE *Moi, je m'appelle La Rose de Shanghai.*

MISS U *Est-ce que vous êtes française?*

MISS CAKE *Pas au'jourd'hui.*

> Let the fruit ripen on the tree
> For if not the meat will harden.
> I'm the peach of the west.
> Chicken is he who does not love me.

> I come from a country named America

MR. R You do?

MISS CAKE I do.

> Chicken is he who does not love me;
> For there's more to the cake than the icing.
> A morsel I'm not, I'm a feast,
> And this not every man knows.
> Remember all the times
> You thought you got a bargain?

MISS U I do.

MISS CAKE

> And it cost you more than it was worth?

MISS I Aha!

MISS CAKE

> That's what we're here for,
> To learn one thing or another;

For on art alone one cannot live.
Chicken is he who does not love me.

Tell me you adore me, and I'll let you go.

ALL   We adore you.

MISS CAKE

I'm the peach of the west, you know,
And a bit of a rebel, just a bit.
And chicken is he, chicken are you all.
I'm not a morsel, I'm a feast,
I'm not a morsel, I'm a feast,
I'm not a morsel, I'm a feast.

MR. R   A toast. . . . A toast. . . .

MR. S   To the ladies. . . . To the ladies. . . .

THEY *all dance.*

ALL

Only four,
Only four
Naked ladies.
Four . . . four . . .
Four naked ladies.

LADIES

Thank you,
Thank you, sir.

The JAILER *enters.*

JAILER   Everybody's under arrest.

105 and 106 freeze in an effort to conceal themselves.

MR. S   No, we're not under arrest, we're frolicking.

MISS I   Oh, what fun!

JAILER   Everybody's under arrest. I'm looking for two prisoners escaped from the penitentiary. And everybody's under arrest until
I find them.

MR. T   Oh, silly man, don't you see we're having fun. Oh joy, joy,
joy.

The LADIES *and* GENTLEMEN *start sitting around the table.*

JAILER   *(Suspiciously)* And why is everybody naked?

MR. S   Only the ladies are naked. The men are in full dress.

The JAILER *looks around.*

JAILER   True . . . true. . . .

HE *goes after* MISS U. MISS U *takes a few little steps away from
him.*

MISS U   *(Pressing her nostrils with her fingers and striking a cherubic
arabesque)* Oh.

JAILER   Well, I may not smell of roses, but when there's a job to do,
I do it. I'm looking for those prisoners and nothing can detract
me from my search.

MISS I *walks past him.* HE *follows her.*

I sense complicity here. *(Looking closely at her buttocks)* Fin-
gerprints perhaps . . .

HE *touches her buttocks;* MISS U *slaps his hand. To* MISS O:

Madam, as an officer of the law I must conduct a search.

MISS O   Oh, stop bringing the street into our lives. You're common.

JAILER   *(to* MISS CAKE*)* Speaking of common, madam, I've seen you.
You look familiar.

MISS CAKE *hits the* JAILER *on the head.* HE *crawls under the table.*

MISS O   *(To* MR. R*)* Let us be irrational.

MR. R *walks away.* SHE *addresses herself to 105 and 106.*

Let's you and me embrace.

105 and 106 are not sure which one SHE *means.* THEY *both start
moving and bump against each other, bow to each other, offer
the way to each other and so on.* THEY *finally reach her with open
arms.*

The moment has passed.

You have, perhaps, made me feel something,
But the moment has passed.
And what is done cannot be undone.
Once a moment passes, it never comes again.

I once had a man who loved me well.
His mouth was smaller than his eye.
But I loved him just the same.
Yes, I loved him just the same.

He said he would kill for me.
And I said, "like, for instance, whom?"
And he said, "like, for instance, you,
Like for instance you."

Sometimes it hurts more than others.
Sometimes it hurts less.
Sometimes it's just the same.
Sometimes it's really just the same.

But never mind that.
No, never mind that.
God gave understanding just to confuse us,
And it's always the same anyway.
It's always the same anyway.

If it's in your path to hurt me,
By all means, do.
But, I beg you, don't go out of your way
Don't go out of your way to do so.

You don't know what to make of me.
But I know what to make of you.
I have nothing to lose,
Or not much, anyway.
But never mind that.
God gave understanding just to confuse us,
And it's always the same anyway.

You have, perhaps, made me feel something,
But the moment has passed.
And what is done cannot be undone.
Once a moment passes, it never comes again.

MISS O *joins the rest at the table.*

MR. T *(Offering* MISS I *a smelling potion)* Have a little philter-
philtre.

MR. R *holds a bunch of grapes over* MISS U *'s mouth while* HE
eats a leg of turkey.

MISS U Oh, how good these grapes are. . . . To the left, Mr. R
. . . a little to the left. . . .

MISS I   Pass the syrup, Mr. S. . . . You pour it. I like the way you pour . . . profusely, Mr. S . . . let it flow. Ahhh.

The JAILER *kisses* MISS U *'s foot.* MR. R *leans over and eats grapes from the same bunch as* MISS I. *The* SERVANT *and the* WAITER *wait on the* GUESTS. MR. R *and* MR. S *offer grapes to* MISS CAKE. SHE *looks at one and then the other.*

MISS CAKE   I seem to be undecided. I'll take both, one from each.

SHE *opens her mouth.* THEY *each push the bottom grape of their bunches in her mouth with the tip of their fingers.* SHE *closes her mouth and* THEY *pull the bunch off.*

MR. R and MR. S   Ahhh . . .

THEY *all begin to yawn and feel drowsy.*

MISS I   Ahh, I feel a breeze.

MR. S *blows in her direction.*

MISS O   Sleep, sweet sleep.

MISS U   *(In a sleepy manner)* I'd like another taste.

MISS I   Have you tasted the melon, Mr. T? It's sweet and ripe. . . .

MR. T   Mommommmom. . . .

MR. S *burps.* THEY *start snoring.* 105 *and* 106 *survey the room.*

105   Can you bear this bliss?

106   Yes!

105   The source of satisfaction is wealth. Isn't it?

106   It is.

105 *and* 106 *start stealing jewels from the* LADIES *and* GENTLE-
MEN. *The* JAILER *notices them and starts walking toward them
stealthily.* 105 *and* 106 *move furtively around the room. The*
JAILER *follows them.*

106   *(Making a gallant gesture)* Après vous.

JAILER   *(Repeating the gesture)* Pas du tout.

106   *(Repeating the gesture)* Je vous en prie.

JAILER   *(Repeating the gesture)* Mon plaisir.

105 and 106   *(Repeating the gesture)* Le nôtre.

JAILER, 105 and 106   *(Sing)*

> Après vous.
> Après vous.
> Pas du tout.
> Je vous en prie.
> Mon plaisir.
> Le nôtre.
> Permettez-moi.
> Notre plaisir.
> Le mien.
> A votre service.
> Au votre.
> Au votre.
> L'age avant la beauté.

The SERVANT *kicks the* JAILER *out the door.* 105 *and* 106 *kiss
her and resume stealing.* THEY *sing while* THEY *take the* MEN*'s
wallets and watches, the* LADIES' *jewelry, the candlesticks, the
silverware, the tablecloth and the chandelier.* THEY *put everything in their sacks.*

105

Can you bear this bliss?

106

No.

105

Can you bear this bliss?

106

Yes.

105 and 106

Eating is a blessing.
Money is a joy.
Drinking is a pleasure,
And Riches a delight.

SERVANT

We've come to one conclusion
That's readily discerned:
A lot of satisfaction
Does away with discontent.

Doesn't it?
A lot of satisfaction
Produces happiness.
And the source of satisfaction
Is wealth.
Isn't it?
All that man possesses
Displaces discontent.

SERVANT   What? What? What? What? What?

105 and 106

> Diamonds and cakes,
> Macaroons and furs
> Dispel discontent.
> Chandeliers and wine,
> Porcelain and lace
> Efface discontent.

106 takes a jewel from MISS CAKE.

MISS CAKE   *(Taking it back)* Oh no you don't.

105, 106 and SERVANT

> Silverware and hats,
> Embroideries and salt,
> Flower pots and yachts,
> Cinnamon and bells,
> And awnings
> And cushions,
> And satins,
> And rings,
> And castles,
> And crackers,
> And things,
> Things,
> Things,
> Things,

105, 106 and the SERVANT *exit as* THEY *continue singing.*

> Things,
> Things . . .

The LADIES *and* GENTLEMEN *begin to stir.*

MISS O   Ah! We have been robbed!

MR. T   Where is my pearl stickpin?

MISS I   Oh, where, where, where?

MR. R   Where is my fur *porte-monnaie?*

MISS U   Where is my ruby tooth?

MR. S   Where is my monogram?

ALL   Where? Where? Where? Where? *(As* THEY *exit)* Where? Where? Where? Where?

SCENE 3

The Street. 105, 106, *and the* SERVANT *enter arm in arm doing a dance step.*

106   Did you really like that party?

THEY *stop dancing.*

106   Yes . . . I liked it.

105   I liked it too. . . .

106   You did?

105   Yes. . . .

106   *(To the* SERVANT*)* Did you?

SHE *thinks a moment.* THEY *resume the dance step and circle the stage.*

SERVANT   You know?

THEY *stop dancing.*

106   What?

SERVANT   To discover what everyone has always known is not important.

106   No, it isn't.

105 *and* 106 *take a step as if to resume the dance.*

SERVANT   However . . .

105   What?

SERVANT   I have just discovered what life is all about.

105   You have?

SERVANT   I have.

> To walk down the street
> With a mean look in my face,
> A cigarette in my right hand
> A toothpick in my left;
> To alternate between the cigarette
> And the toothpick,
> Ah! That's life.
>
> Yes, I have learned from life.
> Every day I've learned some more.
> Every blow has been of use.
> Every joy has been a lesson.
> Yes, I have learned from life.
> What surprises me
> Is that life
> Has not learned from me.

Why? . . . Well. . . . That would be hard to explain. . . . If I
could give you a kiss, perhaps you'd understand.

The SERVANT *gives each a kiss.*

You still don't understand? . . . No?

Well, then,
Because I'm placid as a cow,
As lucid as glass,
As frank as a bald head,
As faithful as a dog.

THEY *start exiting doing the same dance step.*

You see what I mean?

105 and 106 express doubt with their faces and nod. THEY *exit.
The* MOTHER *enters.* SHE *walks slowly across the stage. When*
SHE *reaches mid-stage* SHE *turns to the audience.*

MOTHER   Have you seen my babies? *(Pause)* No? . . . All right.

SHE *exits. There is the sound of a car, brakes, and a crash. The*
INJURED MAN *is hurled on stage. The car is heard starting and
taking off at high speed. 105, 106 and the* SERVANT *enter.* THEY
look the INJURED MAN *over.* THEY *pull the top of their sack
open and give it to the* SERVANT *to hold. 106 takes the* INJURED
MAN*'s wallet, watch, ring, shoes, and jacket, and passes them to
105 who puts them in the sack.* THEY *start tiptoeing away.*

INJURED MAN   Ohh . . .

105, 106 and the SERVANT *stop short.*

Ohhh . . . ohhh . . .

105   *(Still without moving)* What was that?

INJURED MAN   Ohhh . . .

> 105, 106 *and the* SERVANT *tiptoe to the* INJURED MAN. 105 *picks up the* INJURED MAN *'s arm.*

Ohhh . . .

> 105 *drops the arm. There is a short pause.* HE *picks up the other arm.*

Ohhh . . .

> 105 *drops the arm.*

Ohhh . . .

105   He aches.

> THEY *look at each other.* THEY *look at the* INJURED MAN. *The* DRIVER *enters.*

DRIVER   I came back.

INJURED MAN   Ohh. Ohh.

DRIVER   To the scene of the crime.

INJURED MAN   Ohh. Ohh.

DRIVER   I'm a hit-and-run driver.

INJURED MAN   Ohh. Ohh.

DRIVER   I'll kill myself if you die.

INJURED MAN   Ohh. Ohh. I'm cold.

The JAILER *enters.*

JAILER   Have you seen two prisoners escaped from the penitentiary? One tall. The other just a little taller?

105 *and* 106 *lie as injured.*

They wear prisoners' uniforms with the number 105 and 106 on the front and on the back of their jacks.

105 *and* 106 *take off their jackets and put them on the* INJURED MAN. *The number* 105 *is visible on his chest and* 106 *on his back.*

INJURED MAN

Thank you,
Thank you.
You're so nice,
You're so nice.
Thank you,
Thank you.
You're so nice,
You're so nice,
You're so nice.
Thank you,
Oh, thank you.

JAILER   *(Pointing to the* INJURED MAN*)* That's one of them! Get up, 105.

The JAILER *hits the* INJURED MAN *on the stomach. The* INJURED MAN *bends over. The number* 106 *is visible on his back.*

There's the other. Get up, 106. That's them all right. Get up.

DRIVER   Leave him alone. You're kicking the injured man.

JAILER   What do you mean? That's 105 and 106.

DRIVER   Does that look like two people to you? That's the injured man.

105 *and* 106 *begin to shiver.*

INJURED MAN   My friends are cold, too. Someone must have stolen their clothes.

DRIVER   I'll take the clothes off my back to give to your friends. If you die I'll kill myself. *(The* DRIVER *gives his jacket and vest to* 105 *and* 106. HE *shivers)* Now I'm cold.

INJURED MAN   *(Giving one of the jackets to the* DRIVER*)* I have enough for two.

JAILER   Which reminds me of this little woman I used to have. She used to take her clothes off all the time. That was the only thing I liked about her . . . hey! There you are, 105 and 106. *(Taking the* DRIVER *and the* INJURED MAN *by the collar)* Don't tell me you're just one. I see you as plain as day. One and two. I can count. Don't tell me I can't count.

HE *exits with the* DRIVER *and the* INJURED MAN.

SERVANT

Neither probe nor ignore
That the clothes make the man.
Isn't it true that costumes
Change the course of life?

Who can marry a gigolo?
Can you?
Can you?
I can't.

Who can love a businessman?
Can you?
Can you?
I can't.

Who can pity a cop?
Who can reason with a clown?
Who can dance with a priest?
Can you?
Can you?
I can't.

105, 106 and SERVANT

You see, a costume
Can change your life.
Be one and all.
Be each and all.
Transvest,
Impersonate,
'Cause costumes
Change the course
Of life.

The JAILER *re-enters, carrying the prisoners' jackets by the collar.*

JAILER   I'm taking these two prisoners back to jail.

HE *shrugs his shoulders and exits.*

105, 106 and SERVANT

Who can argue with a jailer?
Can you?
Can you?
I can't.

Be one and all.
Be each and all.
Transvest,
Impersonate,
'Cause costumes
Change the course
Of life.

THEY *exit.*

SCENE 4

The Park. 105 *and* 106 *sit on a bench.* THEY *each knit one end of a single scarf. The* SERVANT *sits between them. The* MOTHER *enters.*

MOTHER   I've lost my babies. I've been looking for them for years and I can't find them. Have you seen them?

106   No.

MOTHER   You haven't seen my babies, have you?

SERVANT   No.

MOTHER   They aren't very pretty, but they have beautiful eyes. I lost my babies right here. Have you seen them?

105 and 106   No.

MOTHER

Have you seen my babies?
I've been looking for them for years,
And I can't find them.

Have you seen them?
Have you seen them?
Have you seen them?

Have you seen two little angels?
Have you? With skin soft like feathers
In diapers still.

Have you seen them?
Have you seen them?
Have you seen them?

Have you seen those sweet angels?
Have you seen them . . .

The MOTHER *looks closely at* 105 *and* 106.

No. . . . My babies were pretty. These are not my babies. *(*SHE *looks again)* No. These are big, ugly and old. Mine were this big. *(*SHE *indicates the size of an infant)* And pretty. . . . Bye.

105 and 106   Bye.

The MOTHER *exits.*

106   Hmm. Big, ugly and old . . .

105   Well, we could be younger.

The MOTHER *re-enters and watches* 105 *and* 106 *from behind the bushes.*

106   True.

105   We could be prettier.

106   Not true.

105   We could be smaller.

106   Don't want to be.

105 and 106

> It's to age
> That we owe
> What we are.
>
> In fact we're grateful
> For the passing of time.
> It's only fitting
> We should be grateful
> For the passing of time.
> 'Cause
> Without growth
> We'd not be
> What we are.

MOTHER   What are you?

> THEY *pose for her.* THEY *point to themselves from head to toe.*
> THEY *do a turn.* THEY *do a tap step.*

105 and 106

> We are
> All that we are.
> From head to toe.
>
> Once it's thoroughly thought through
> We should realize
> It's only appropriate
> We should be attracted
> To the passing of time,
> Attracted to the passing of time.
> 'Cause it's to age

That we owe what we are,
And without it
We'd not be
What we are.

MOTHER   It's distressing to get old.

106   Well, you are bound to get older. . . .

105   If you're going to be alive.

The LADIES *and* GENTLEMEN *walk in, led by* MR. S, *who scans the floor for footprints.* THEY *walk by* 105, 106 *and the* SERVANT *without noticing them.*

MR. S   They went this way. Follow me. I took a course in trails, tracks and clues. *(*HE *discovers* MISS U*'s foot)* Oh, what pretty feet you have, Miss U.

MISS U   I do?

MR. T   Feet? Where? Oh. . . .

MR. S   Dainty.

MR. T   Hm. Delicious. *(Lifting her skirt)* Let's see your ankle, Miss U. Oh, it's pretty.

MISS U   Mr. R, wouldn't you like to admire my feet? Each toe has a personality all its own.

MR. R   Oh, I've seen them.

MISS U   You cad. *(To* MR. S *and* MR. T*)* Who am I?

MR. S and MR. T   The queen!

MISS U   And what are my virtues?

MR. S *and* MR. T *lift her up on their shoulders.*

MR. S and MR. T   You are flighty! You are fickle! And you are wicked!

MISS U   That's right.

THEY *put her down.* MISS U *walks to* MR. R. HE *turns his back to her.*

You rascal.

Capricious as I am, and fickle,
In spite of my renowned restlessness,
In spite of my noted changeability;
My versatility, my spirit of adventure,
One day because of your winning ways.
I gave you all I had.
And you in your typical fashion,
Conceited, flippant, and complacent,
Just threw it all away,
Just threw it all away.
You heel! You cad!
You treated me the way I treated others.
You scoundrel!
How dare you bring shame to my life? Shame . . . shame.

One day, because of your amorous claims,
I learned that pleasure
Does not need fabrication;
That true love catches you by surprise.
But you, confirmed egotist,
You were just playing games.

You insisted on re-enacting
A moment from your past;
Either a moment that you lived

Or a moment that you imagined.
You heel! You were just playing games. Shame . . . shame. . . .

I am conceited, flippant and deceitful,
And I am flightly, frivolous, and vain.
And you, scoundrel,
You treated me the way I treated others.
Just who do you think you are?

In spite of my reputation
As a lady without heart
I gave my heart to you.
You heel . . .
And here I am.
I've lost my heart to you.

Unaccustomed as I am
To asking a man for his favor,
I'm asking you,
Come . . . come . . . come. . .
I'm helpless without you.

MR. R *walks to* MISS U. THEY *kiss. Immediately after,* MR. R
touches MISS I*'s face and blows her a kiss.* MISS U *punches* MR.
R *in the stomach.* MR. R *falls.* MR. T *and* MR. S *carry him off
followed by* MISS O, MISS I, MISS U, *and the* MOTHER.

SERVANT   Ahhhh. Riches made them dumb.

105   Who?

SERVANT   All of them. Mr. R, Mr. S, Mr. T, Miss I, Miss O, Miss
       U.

105   Really?

SERVANT   Yes, money made them dumb.

106   Did it? How dumb.

SERVANT   Very dumb. Money makes you dumb.

106   Naw . . .

SERVANT   Yes! . . . I'll show you.

SHE *puts on a bracelet, a necklace and a brooch.* SHE *imitates the speech of the* LADIES *and* GENTLEMEN.

If someone scrubs the pot. Perhaps it will get shiny. I'm neither this, nor that. Only exactly what I think I am. That is, if you think I'm frank, frank, frank.

SHE *reaches for more jewels.* 105 *and* 106 *begin to dress her.* THEY *drape a lace tablecloth around her, hang the silverware around her waist and put the rest of the jewelry on her. At the end of the song* THEY *put the chandelier on her head as a crown.*

Is it time yet to be naked?
Oh no no no no no, oh no.
It might be a little indiscreet
To take off my clothes before three.
Aah . . . aah . . . aah . . .

It is now time to get dressed.
Dress, dress, dress, dress, dress me.
It is time to put on my clothes.
Aah . . . aah . . . aah . . .

In my life I've made some errors.
Errors one and two and three,
Four, five, six,
Seven, eight, nine, ten.
Wonderful errors. Marvelous errors.
From a to z.

I used to be an ordinary girl
With a delicate soul.
Now I'm just ordinary.
Where did my soul go?
Aah . . . aah . . . aah
Where did it go?
Where did my soul go?

Someone has mentioned my name.
But who is it he speaks of?
You see I'm neither this nor that,
Neither this nor that.
And I'm not free to love.

Someone has mentioned my name
But I'm neither this nor that.
And I've forgotten who I am,
I've forgotten who I am.
But I can, I can, I can rhyme,
Yme,* yme, yme, yme, yme,
I can, I can, I can rhyme,
Yme, yme, yme, yme, yme.

Why have you not crowned me yet.
I'm neither this nor that
But I can rhyme.
I can rhyme
Yme, yme, yme, yme, yme.

THEY *crown her.*

I can rhyme
Yme, yme, yme, yme, yme.
You see what I mean?

_____
*Pronounced ime.

105   Not really.

106   *shakes his head.*

SERVANT   *(In an attempt to convince them)*

Yme yme yme yme yme yme
Rhyme.

It's also bad for your health. *(SHE sneezes)*

106   Are you rich, dear? You seem to have a cold.

SERVANT   I used to be poor. Very, very poor. But now, I'm very, very, very, very rich. *(SHE sneezes)*

105   You are?

SERVANT   Yes.

106   Watch out you don't lose your brains. Remember, riches make you dumb. Ho ho ho.

105   And you are even beginning to imagine things. Ho ho.

106

Riches make you dumb.

105

Yme, yme, yme, rhyme.

SERVANT

I can rhyme.

106 *places the sack on the floor next to the* SERVANT, *while* 106 *picks her up and stands her on the sack. Now* SHE *is part of their*

loot. *The* JAILER *watches from a corner.* THEY *pull the sack over the* SERVANT's *head, carry her on their shoulders and exit.*

ACT II / SCENE 1

The Battlefield. There is the sound of bombs. The lights flash on and off. SOLDIERS I *and* II *lie on the floor. Their heads, arms, and torsos are wrapped in bandages.* 105 *and* 106 *run across the stage.* THEY *still carry the* SERVANT. *The* JAILER *follows them.* HE *stops when* HE *sees the* SOLDIERS.

JAILER   There you are, 105 and 106, you're digging. Your disguise does not deceive me. I'd recognize you miles away. I'm a smart man and your tricks are puerile.

Bomb.

I think I'll watch from afar. This time they're playing with dynamite and a man can get hurt with that.

Bomb. HE *exits.*

SOLDIER I   John . . .

SOLDIER II   What?

SOLDIER I   Did you get drafted?

SOLDIER II   Drafted!

SOLDIER I   Did you volunteer?

SOLDIER II   For what?

SOLDIER I   To get the bombs dropped on you.

SOLDIER II   No, I didn't.

SOLDIER I   How did they get you?

SOLDIER II   I was going home from work when someone said: "Hey, soldier!" and I made the mistake to look.

SOLDIER I   You volunteered then.

SOLDIER II   Why?

SOLDIER I   Because you looked.

SOLDIER II   Gosh! I shouldn't have looked.

SOLDIER I   Well, they get you anyway, whether you look or not.

SOLDIER II   How did they get you?

SOLDIER I   I got drafted. When the man said "Hey, soldier," I kept walking. But he hit me on the head, told me to drop my pants, spread my cheeks, threw me on a barber chair, and here I am. . . . They didn't even let me face the mirror.

SOLDIER II   That's tough.

SOLDIER I   John, we used to have a good time, didn't we?

SOLDIER II   Yes, remember the time we got in trouble by the fountain?

SOLDIER I   *You* got in trouble.

SOLDIER II   I was a little drunk. And there was a cop standing in the corner. And I said to him "Hey, flatfoot." . . . Ha ha ha ha ha. . . . It was a nice evening.

SOLDIER I   John . . .

SOLDIER II   What?

SOLDIER I   Do you think we're going to win the war?

SOLDIER II   We might.

SOLDIER I   How can we? We don't even have guns.

SOLDIER II   Only bandages.

SOLDIER I   What can we do with bandages?

SOLDIER II   Just wait till we get hit, I guess.

> *A bomb falls. At the same time* 105 *and* 106 *are hurled on stage. Their heads and torsos are wrapped in bandages.* SOLDIERS I *and* II *fall to the ground. Another bomb falls.* 105 *and* 106 *huddle up to the* SOLDIERS. THEY *are silent and motionless for a while.*

SOLDIER I   John . . .

SOLDIER II   What?

SOLDIER I   Are you alive?

SOLDIER II   Yes. I'm just wounded. . . . And you?

SOLDIER I   Just wounded. . . . *(Pause)* John . . .

SOLDIER II   What?

> SOLDIER I *points to* 105 *and* 106. SOLDIER II *turns his head cautiously.*

Who are they?

SOLDIER I   *(Pointing to* SOLDIER II, *himself and all around)* Same thing. . . . Enlisted. . . . *(To* 105 *and* 106*)* How did they get you?

106   We were walking down the street and we heard someone say, "Hey, soldier."

SOLDIER I   And you looked.

SOLDIER II   You shouldn't have looked.

SOLDIER I   Well, they get you anyway. I didn't look, but they hit me on the head, threw me on the barber chair, and here I am . . . waiting for the bombs. . . . *(Pause)* John . . .

SOLDIER II   What?

SOLDIER I   In case I don't make it, drop this in the mail, will you?

SOLDIER II   What is it?

SOLDIER I   A letter. Can't you see it's a letter?

SOLDIER II   What does it say?

SOLDIER I *takes the letter out of the envelope and sings.*

SOLDIER I

"Sidney N. Phelps, Director.
Dining, sleeping, and parlor car,
Penn Central, Long Island City,
New York, one one one o one.

"Mr. Phelps,
On Tuesday, March seventeenth,
On board The Boston Colonial
Of the Penn Central Railroad
I had the worst hamburger
I ever had;

Served to me on dining car
Four four seven four four.
Mr. Phelps, I've had
Bad hamburgers before,
But that was the worst
I ever had."

SOLDIER II   That's awful. I'll mail it for you.

HE reaches for the letter but is distracted by the MAYOR *and* MISS CAKE *'s entrance.* HE *carries a picnic basket.* SHE *wears a shawl.* THEY *walk through serenely and gallantly.*

MAYOR   My rose, is it too cool for you?

MISS CAKE   Don't mention it.

The SOLDIERS, 105 *and* 106 *watch them exit.* SOLDIER II *reaches for the letter again.*

SOLDIER I   I don't really want it mailed.

SOLDIER II   Why not?

SOLDIER I   I don't care about the hamburger.

SOLDIER II   You don't?

SOLDIER I   No.

SOLDIER II   Why did you write the letter?

SOLDIER I   I was angry . . . at Madeline.

SOLDIER II   You wrote a letter about a hamburger because you were angry at Madeline?

SOLIDER 1   Yes.

When Madeline told me it was all off
I took The Boston Colonial,
And as the train pulled off
I looked to see if my Madeline was there,
But she wasn't.
Oh, Madeline. Oh, Madeline
Why weren't you there?
Why weren't you there?

Bomb. The MOTHER *enters.*

MOTHER   Have you seen my babies?

The SOLDIERS, 105 *and* 106 *shake their heads.*

They were round and tender. . . . They only spoke two words
. . . poles apart. . . . Let me see if I can remember. . . .
North-South. . . . No, that's not it. . . . Well, take any two words
and say they were it. Have you seen them?

THEY *shake their heads.*

They had small teeth. Like little grains of rice. And just two
. . . in front. . . . You haven't seen them?

THEY *shake their heads.* THE MOTHER *exits singing "Two Little
Angels" sotto-voce. The* MAYOR *and* MISS CAKE *enter.*

MAYOR   Ah, there you are. I seem to have bypassed you. *(To* MISS
CAKE*)* Here is the platoon, my lily. We bypassed them.

MISS CAKE   Yes. . . . This is where they are . . . and were.

The SERVANT *enters, running.* SHE *carries the loot bag. The*
JAILER *follows her.* THEY *circle the* SOLDIERS *twice. The* JAILER
changes direction and grabs the SERVANT *as* SHE *runs toward*

him. SHE *throws the loot bag up in the air.* 106 *catches it and throws it to* 105 *as the* JAILER *goes toward him.*

MAYOR   Oh, what's happening? Why all the running?

The bag goes from hand to hand until it falls in the MAYOR*'s hands.*

Oh, a donation for the orphanage . . . from the troops. How timely. I was just thinking I need a new team of horses . . . for my new carriage.

HE *starts giving the bag to the* JAILER.

Here, take this to my house. Never mind, I'll do it myself.

HE *gives the* JAILER *the picnic basket.*

Take this. Go find a nice spot for the picnic, with flowers and a view. And take my damsel to it. Make sure it's a shady spot. The sun makes her blush.

MISS CAKE   Flush.

JAILER   Flush sounds better. I'm sure this lady never blushed.

The SERVANT *tries to take the bag from the* MAYOR. HE *threatens her with the back of his hand. The* LADIES *and* GENTLEMEN *enter in the manner of people at a garden party.*

MAYOR   What now? Review the troops. Att-ent-ion. There you are . . . standing at attention. Fine bunch. They jump at my command.

THEY ALL *jump slightly.*

Ha ha. That's the spirit. Let's see . . . *(Referring to* MISS 1*)* That's a nice posture, Sergeant. *(Giving her a slap on the back)* Good boy . . . good boy. Splendid, get his name. *(To* MISS O*)* That's a nice uniform, officer, where did you have it made? Shipshape. *(HE kisses* MISS O *on both cheeks)* You can't tell the men from the women nowadays. But it doesn't matter . . . it does not matter as long as they can shoot. Shoot. Shoot. Nothing wrong with you boys. *(Looking at* MISS U*)* Hm, that's a good cannon ball. Yes, shipshape. Everything's in good form. Lucky stiffs. Shoot. Shoot.

Bomb.

Ooops. Don't shoot your captain now. Shoot to the side. Ha ha. Yes, sir, pretty field you have here, roses and fireworks. Lucky stiffs, you can have a picnic any time you want. . . . Look at those guns. Great guns. Rifles. That's what you call them.

Bomb.

Ooops. What's that noise? I didn't know it was the Fourth of July. . . . Neither did I. Hm. I'm sure I brought someone with me. Where is my damsel?

MISS CAKE   Yooo hoooo. I'm here.

MAYOR   There you are of course.

The MAYOR *goes to* MISS CAKE.

MISS U   Rompous-mompus-gambol-mumble!

The music for "Spring is Here" starts.

MAYOR   Hmmm. I smell chocolate pudding. . . . Where is it?

HE *stands abruptly and runs after the* SERVANT.

LADIES   Mompus-mumble-rompous-gambol!

The JAILER *and the* MAYOR *bump against each other.* THEY *start dancing together.* MISS CAKE *dances on the tablecloth. The* LA-DIES *and* GENTLEMEN *start undoing the* SOLDIER'S *head bandages.*

LADIES and GENTLEMEN   Spring is here!

LADIES

Ahaa ahaa ahaa
Arbutus are here,
And spring beauties.
Ohoo ohoo ohoo
It's springtime,
And hepaticas are blooming.

The LADIES *and* GENTLEMEN *dance around the* SOLDIERS *using their head bandages as ribbons around a Maypole.*

LADIES and GENTLEMEN

I see a bride,
Oohoohoo hoohoohoo
I see a bride in white.
Oohoohoo hoohoohoo

SOLDIER I   Oh, please don't.

LADIES and GENTLEMEN

I see a lady,
I see two,
I see a groom behind a tree.
Oohoohoo hoohoohoo

SOLDIER I   Don't do that.

Simultaneously with:

SOLDIER II   Please don't.

LADIES and GENTLEMEN

> Come out, come out
> Wherever you are.
> Come out, come out
> Wherever you are.

LADIES   Those who give will get of nature's bounty through the year.

SOLDIER I and SOLDIER II   Oh.

> *The* MOTHER *starts hitting the* DANCERS.

MOTHER   Leave them alone . . .

LADIES and GENTLEMEN

> I see a bride,
> Oohoohoo hoohoohoo.
> I see a bride in white,
> Oohoohoo hoohoohoo.

MOTHER   Leave them alone. Let go.

LADIES and GENTLEMEN

> I see a lady,
> I see two.
> I see a groom
> Behind a tree,
> Oohoohoo hoohoohoo.
>
> Apples,
> Peaches,

Pumpkin pie.
I see you,
I see you,
Anyone I see is it.

LADIES Look down a well reflected in a mirror. And you'll see your
future spouse's face.

SOLDIER I Oh Madeline.

LADIES   GENTLEMEN

Ready or not here I come.   Come out, come out
Ready or not here I come.   Come out, come out

SOLDIER I

I looked to see if my Madeline
Was there.
But she wasn't.
Oh, Madeline, Madeline, Madeline.
Why weren't you there.

LADIES *and* GENTLEMEN O, what a fierce and fiery fiesta.

SERVANT, 105, 106   LADIES, GENTLEMEN

Riches made them dumb   I see a lady
Riches made them dumb   I see two.

MOTHER Let them go.

MAYOR Come to my house everyone. I have plenty of wine, and you
people are a jolly bunch.

The DANCERS *exit as they sing the following:*

DANCERS

> Après vous,
> Après vous,
> Pas du tout.
> Je vous en prie.
> Mon plaisir.
> Le nôtre.
> Permettez-moi.
> Notre plaisir.
> Le mien.
> A votre service.
> Au votre.
> Au votre.
> L'age avant la beauté.

The MOTHER, 105, 106 *and the* SERVANT *go to the* SOLDIERS. *The* MOTHER *and the* SERVANT *hold them in their arms while* 105 *and* 106 *take off their bandages.*

MOTHER   Here. I have something you'll like. *(SHE looks in her pockets)* Oh, I forgot to bring it. *(SHE looks again)* I always have something in my pockets. Well, I'll tell you a story. . . . There was a man . . . a very wise man who wanted to conquer pain. He tried and tried but he couldn't find a way. . . . One day he went fishing just to distract himself from this thought that occupied his mind. . . . He caught one fish and then another . . . and as he sat there waiting for the next fish to bite, he suddenly said, "I got it! You conquer pain the way you catch a fish. When pain bites you don't look away. You pull it toward you. And when it's right on top of you, and it starts flapping, and almost knocking you down, that's when you have it conquered, because it's out of the water." Yes, that's what he said.

105 and 106

> When I was born I opened my eyes,
> And when I looked around I closed them;
> And when I saw how people get kicked in the head,

And kicked in the belly, and kicked in the groin,
I closed them.
My eyes are closed but I'm carefree.
Ho ho ho, ho ho ho, I'm carefree.

105

A poor man has fifty problems every day,
Fifty problems upon opening his eyes,
Fifty problems every minute of the day.
And life is sour.
One thing a poor man has,
That a rich man doesn't have,
Is fifty problems every day.

When a wound is open
And the guts are hanging out,
It hurts.
And it hurts as much
When a man's life
Is dark and narrow.

A poor man doesn't know
Where his pain comes from.
There is a dark wall,
And a closed door,
And a dirty old room,
And he doesn't know how he got there.

A poor man's life is sour
And he doesn't know
Who made it so.

106

A poor man has to do what he's told.
He doesn't know just why he does it.
He just has to do what he's told.

Do the dirty work.
Get off the street.
It's you who has to fight the war.

He gets kicked in the head,
And kicked in the belly,
And kicked in the groin.

I know what madness is.
It's not-knowing how another man feels.
A madman has never been
In another man's shoes.

Madness is lack of compassion,
And there's little compassion
In the world.

It's only stupid things
That make a madman feel sure:
Money, power, adulation;
Never just being alive,
Having two feet on the ground,
And having heart to give.

105 and 106

When I was born I opened my eyes,
And when I looked around I closed them;
And when I saw how people get kicked in the head,
And kicked in the belly, and kicked in the groin,
I closed them.
My eyes are closed but I'm carefree.
Ho ho ho, ho ho ho, I'm carefree.

The SOLDIERS *feel their healed bodies.*

SOLDIER II   I feel better.

SOLDIER I   I do too.

SOLDIER II   Let's go to the Mayor's party.

MOTHER   I don't want to go to the Mayor's party.

SOLDIER II   Why not?

MOTHER   I don't like him.

SOLDIER II *beckons the* SERVANT. SHE *shakes her head.*

SOLDIER II   *(To* 105 *and* 106*)* There'll be wine there.

THEY *shake their heads.* HE *goes to* SOLDIER I *and punches him lightly.* SOLDIER I *shakes his head. The music to* "Why Not" *starts.* SOLDIER II *starts dancing.* HE *turns to the* MOTHER.

Come . . .

HE *leads the* MOTHER *in a simple dance.*

SOLDIER I, II, *the* SERVANT *and the* MOTHER

La la la
La la la
La la la
La la la

HE *beckons the* SERVANT *once more.*

SERVANT

Why not? Why not?
Let's go and have some fun
Why not?
If we can dance and have some fun;
If there's free wine.
We're a jolly bunch.

The MOTHER *and* SOLDIER II *start exiting doing the same dance step.* SOLDIER I *and the* SERVANT *join them.*

SOLDIER I, II, *the* SERVANT *and the* MOTHER

Why not? Why not?
Why not?
Why not!

105 and 106 follow them. THEY *are downcast.*

SCENE 2

The Mayor's Drawing Room. The MAYOR *sits on a high chair. A stethoscope hangs from his neck. The* JAILER *and* MISS CAKE *stand by his sides. The* REST *enter in the order* THEY *left the previous scene.*

MAYOR   Welcome. . . . Welcome. . . . I am about to entertain. Whoever is not amused will be sent to the common cell.

JAILER   Hear, hear. The show is about to start.

MAYOR   Have any of you ever heard the story of the rabbit and the turtle?

ALL   Yes.

MAYOR   You see, it goes like this: There was once a rabbit who said to the turtle: "Run fast. Run fast, or I'll win the race." "I'll run slowly," said the turtle, "and win the race." "If that is the case, I'll take a rest," said the rabbit. "Why?" said the turtle. "To give you an advantage," said the rabbit. "Who are you to give me advantages?" said the turtle. And so on . . . and so on . . . and so on. Whoever doesn't laugh will be sent to the common cell.

THEY *all laugh reluctantly.*

Good. Now the party's over. Let me see what time it is. *(Looking at his watch)* Too late! Everybody's under arrest for keeping me up so late. Wait, you've been reprieved. My watch stopped. It must be earlier than I thought. Or later. Amuse yourselves. I give the best parties in town. I don't? Who said that? I must be hearing things again. No one would dare say I don't give the best parties in town. Now, who has some mighty good entertainment?

MR. R, MR. S *and* MR. T *walk to the center in a vaudevillian manner.*

MR. R   This is my son. *(Apologetically)* He needs a haircut.

MR. S   What he needs is a new face.

MR. R, MR. S *and* MR. T *laugh heartily.*

MAYOR   Pretty dull. Pretty dull. I have seen better entertainment than that. You better do something funny, or I'll tell you another story.

MR. R *steps forward.*

MR. R

Whenever my fingers went like this,
I said: "Hell, my fingers always go like that."
Until one day somebody said to me:
"How original it is that your fingers go like that."

Since then, every time my fingers go like this,
I say: "Look at my fingers go like that.
How original it is that my fingers go like this."
One of these days I'll sell them.

THEY *applaud.*

MAYOR   That's nothing! I wouldn't buy your fingers if you paid me. Why, I remember the days when I could do all kinds of things with my fingers and my mother used to say to me, "Why Jennifer, you're being salacious." Ha ha.

THEY *all laugh reluctantly.*

Who's next?

MR. T *takes out a song sheet.* HE *gets the key from the piano and sings:*

MR. T

> It is true I told you I would love you
> And I never did.
> But remember, I'm forgetful,
> Little fool.
> Longings are like vapor.
> They go as they come.
> And remember, little fool,
> I'm forgetful.
>
> Both my wife's and my mistress' name is Kate.
> One day, while I made love to Kate, my wife,
> I thought of my sweet mistress Kate.
> In a moment of passion and confusion,
> I said: "Kate, dear Kate, oh, Kate."
> My wife, hearing me speak my mistress' name,
> Said harsh words to me, and put me on the street.
> Is that fair, I ask you, is that fair?
>
> It is true, I told you I would love you,
> And I never did.
> But remember, I'm forgetful,
> Little fool.

ALL

> Longings are like vapor.
> They go as they come.

MR. T

> And remember, little fool,
> I'm forgetful.

> THEY *all applaud. The* SERVANT *does a dance to the accompaniment of the "Czardas."* OTHERS *play instruments, do head stands, kazatskis, and different tricks according to the actor's ability.*

MAYOR   No good. No good. That's common and ordinary. I'm a poet and a scholar. Let's hear some poetry.

105   Miss Cake?

MISS CAKE   Yes, Mr. 105.

105   What do you aim at in your work?

MISS CAKE   Magic.

106   Do you always achieve it?

MISS CAKE   Yes. Once in a while.

106   You don't mean always, then.

MISS CAKE   Yes, I do.

105   Explain.

MISS CAKE   In mathematical terms, if the impossible is ever achieved, it becomes always. That is how eternity is conceived.

MAYOR   That makes sense. But it's not poetry. Go back to your cake.
Now, this is poetry.

A petunia is a flower like a begonia.
You fry begonia like you fry sausage.
Sausage and battery is a crime.
Monkeys crime trees.
Tree is a crowd.
The cock crowd and made a noise.
You have a noise on your face, also two eyes.
The opposite of ayes is nays.
A horse nays and has a colt.
You go to bed with a colt,
And wake up with double petunia.

Whoever doesn't laugh will be sent to the common cell.

ALL *except* 105 *and* 106 *sing the* "Laughing Song." *The* MAYOR
uses his stethoscope to make sure THEY *are all laughing. At the
end of the song* HE *reaches* 105 *and* 106. *To the* JAILER:

Take them away.

As the JAILER *takes* 105 *and* 106 *away, the* MOTHER *takes a few
steps toward them.*

MOTHER   Don't take my children away.

Does anyone understand a mother's love?
Except a mother?
Does a father understand a mother's love?
Except a good father?
Does anyone understand a mother's love?
Except a son, or a grandfather, or an uncle?

ALL   Everyone.

MOTHER *(Recitative)*

Then do you know that one autumn afternoon
My children disappeared and that that very
Autumn afternoon my life ended?

The JAILER *re-enters with* 105 *and* 106.

JAILER I went the wrong way. That's the kitchen. *(*HE *walks in the opposite direction)*

MOTHER Oh . . . I must kill myself.

The MOTHER *pantomimes reaching for a knife and stabbing herself.* SHE *falls to the ground.*

MAYOR Marvelous . . . marvelous. That's good entertainment. Do it again.

The MOTHER *stands and repeats the same motions.*

Marvelous. Now the party is over. Let me see what time it is. Too late! Everybody's under arrest for keeping me up so late. Good night. That was mighty good entertainment. The old lady's on the ball.

The JAILER *takes everyone to jail. The* MAYOR *waves.*

I must remember that.

HE *tries to remember the* MOTHER *'s movements. The lights fade.*

SCENE 3

The Cell. It is empty. There is the sound of voices. ALL *except the* MAYOR *enter.*

JAILER   The ladies are to come with me to the next cell . . . one at a time. It's too crowded here.

MISS O   Yes, it's too crowded here. I am not having fun.

MR. T   Don't push, Miss I. There is no place to go. *(To* MR. S*)* You are stepping on my toe.

MR. S   Who said that being arrested could be fun?

MISS I   Well, it's not all that it's made up to be. It's a bore.

MISS U   I like it.

MR. R   She likes it. Why do you like it?

MISS U   It's different.

MR. R   You're sticking your elbow in my back, Miss O.

MISS O   I can't help it. I'm being pushed.

MR. R   Well, don't bend your arm. Keep it straight.

   MISS O *straightens her arm.*

MR. S   Oops. Who did that?

MR. T   I'm going home. Make way.

MISS O   Me too.

JAILER   You can't go home. You're under arrest.

   MR. T *and* MISS O *exit through the hole.*

MR. S   Little man, step aside.

The JAILER *steps aside.* ALL *except the* MOTHER, *the* SERVANT, 105 *and* 106 *begin to exit.*

MR. R Let's call Mr. Lipschitz..

MR. S Let's play croquet. At night you don't know if the ball went under the wicket.

MISS O Oh, let's play it on my lawn. I don't even have a set.

MISS I Fickle. . . .

The JAILER *exits through the door and locks it.*

JAILER Well, whoever is left is under arrest.

HE *exits.*

SERVANT Sure. *(Pause)* Well . . . I'll go now. . . .

MOTHER Where will you go?

SERVAMT I don't know . . . I'll go for a walk.

MOTHER Will you be all right?

SERVANT Yes, it's almost morning. The city is quiet now.

MOTHER Be careful.

SERVANT I'll be careful. *(To* 105 *and* 106*)* Good night, friends.

105 and 106 Good night.

SERVANT I'll be seeing you.

105 and 106 Would you like us to go with you?

SERVANT   No. I . . . It's okay. I'd like to be alone . . . and think.

105 and 106   We'll see you soon. . . .

SERVANT   Real soon.

The door opens for her. SHE *steps out of the cell and turns to wave.* THEY *wave back.* She *exits.*

MOTHER   Well, it's time to go to sleep now.

105 and 106   Yes.

MOTHER   Did you have a good time, my children?

105 and 106   Yes.

MOTHER   Did you find evil?

105 and 106   No.

MOTHER   Good night, then. Sleep well. You'll find it some other time.

105 and 106   Good night.

The MOTHER *rocks them to sleep.*

MOTHER

> I saw a man lying in the street,
> Asleep and drunk, ‑
> He had not washed his face.
> He held his coat closed with a safety pin
> And I thought, and I thought
> Thank God, I'm better than he is.
> Yes, thank God, I'm better than he.

I have to live with my own truth,
I have to live with it.
You live with your own truth,
I cannot live with it.
I have to live with my own truth,
Whether you like it or not,
Whether you like it or not.

There are many poor people in the world,
Whether you like it or not.
There are many poor people in the world.
But I'm not one of them.
I'm not one of them.
Someone's been stealing my apples
But I'm not one of them,
I'm not one of them.

I know everything.
Half of it I really know,
The rest I make up,
The rest I make up.
Some things I'm sure of,
Of other things I'm too sure,
And of others I'm not sure at all.
People believe everything they hear,
Not what they see, not what they see.
People believe everything they hear;
But me, I see everything.
Yes, I see everything.

The saddest day of my life was the day
That I pitied a despicable man.
And I've been sad ever since,
Yes, I've been sad ever since.
I'd like to go where a human being
Is not a strange thing,
Is not a strange thing.

When I go, no one will water my plants.
When I go, no one will water my plants.
No one . . . no one . . . no one . . .

Yes, my children, you'll find evil . . . some other time. . . . Good
night.

SHE *exits.*

105 and 106   Good night.

All is well in the city.
People do what they want.
They can go to the park.
They can sleep all they want.
And for those who have no cake,
There's plenty of bread.

Appendix

The two following scenes were performed in the Off-Broadway production of *Promenade* and were subsequently deleted by the author. Following MISS I's speech on page 221 ("Pass the syrup, Mr. S . . .") and replacing the subsequent dialogue through the beginning of the jewel theft:

MR. S   Let me eat the ice cream from your hands, Miss U.

MISS U *gives him some.*

Both hands, Miss U . . . both hands . . . the left and the right.

MR. R *offers bunches of grapes to* ROSITA. SHE *looks at one and then the other.*

ROSITA   I seem to be undecided. I'll take both, one from each.

SHE *does so.* MR. T *offers* MISS I *a flower.*

MR. T   What would you like?

MISS I   Nothing for me.

MR. T   A flower perhaps.

MISS I   Not even a flower.

MR. T   Can you refuse this unusual forget-me-not? Look, it's minis-cule.

SHE *refuses it.*

She loves me. She loves me . . . not.

MISS I *(Sings)*

I was offered a flower
And I didn't take it.
I had to wait for it too long . . . too long.

If I had been offered a field of flowers
I wouldn't have taken it,
For I was made to wait too long.

Now it comes . . . now it comes. . .
When all my joy is gone . . . all my joy is gone.

If it was to teach me to be patient
That you took the flowers,
The morning sun,
Your youthful laughter,
Your graceful body,
Your tender looks,
If it was to teach me to be patient
You did teach it to me . . . you did . . . ah . . .
I am patient but all my joy is gone.

If you wanted to teach me to be wise
The lesson was bad
There is no wisdom without joy.

Don't laugh now
Not now . . . not now . . .
Don't cry now . . . later
Wait till later.
I am patient but all my joy is gone.

SHE *rejects the flower a final time and moves away to sit.* MR. T
falls asleep. 105 *and* 106 *sneak around the room, enjoying the
surroundings.*

105   Can you bear this bliss?

106   No.

105   Can you bear this bliss?

106   Yes.

105   The source of satisfaction is wealth. Isn't it?

106   It is.

  105 *and* 106 *start stealing jewels from the* GUESTS. *The* MAYOR
  enters.

MAYOR   Good evening! You needn't have waited for me *(*HE *hangs
his cape on* 105 *and* 106*)* I wouldn't have minded if you had
had a little fun before I came. How do you do, Miss O, you
look ravishing. Where is your husband? Oh, there he is. *(To*
MR. T*)* He's dyed his hair blonde—I like it! I see you're beginning to have fun. Yes, I know it's hard to get things going
without me. But you should have tried. You should have tried
. . . The life of the party. Yes, sir, ever since I was a little boy
. . . whether I try or not. My mother used to say to me, "Come,
Jennifer, come and sing for the guests." *(Taking a glass—mime)*
Let's have some wine. It might make me jolly or it might make
me sleepy. Who knows. Who knows. Ahh, there. I feel very
sleepy. I think I'll do a dance. *(Looking at the* SERVANT*)* Well,
look what we have here. *(*HE *puts his finger to her and then puts
the finger to his mouth)* Chocolate pudding, not enough salt.
Hmmm. Well, that's enough merriment for one night. Have to
go see what the chickens are doing. Cackle, cackle, cackle, that's
all they do. But still I have to go see what they're doing. Duty
before pleasure. Where is my horse. There, as usual, sleeping
under the table. *(Going to the* JAILER*)* Get up, Geronimo. Let's
go for a ride. Let's go see if Miss Rodriguez is still receiving
guests.

JAILER I found them, Mayor-Captain . . . I found them. They were digging.

MAYOR *(Riding the* JAILER*)* Fine thing to do at this hour of the night. I only dig in the morning. That's the only time to dig. Yippie-i-ay, Geronimo. That was a fine ride, little horsey. I'll give you a lump of sugar as soon as I get a chance. Where is Rosita? Rosita, I'm here. Make room for me. I had some wine and I'm feeling very jolly.

This morning I watered my garden, Rosita,
And I gave each rose a name.
Rosa Rosita Rosa Rose
Rosita Rosa Rose Rose,
Rosita Rodriguez.
I gave each rose your name.

Rosita Rodriguez,
Each one of my roses
Is named after you.
Rosita Rodriguez.
And my lilies and my daisies
Are also named after you.
Rosita Rodriguez.

I call my lilies roses, Rosita,
Because every bloom is you.
I call my daisies Rosa, Rosita,
And they seem to know they're you.

Open your window, Rosita,
There's a party here for you.
My favorite jewel, my favorite jewel,
The air wants to carry my song to you.
Rosita, the azaleas
Are blooming just for you.

Come to your window,
Rosita.
My song is delirious.
Rosita my rose,
Put my verses in repose.

Rosita Rodriguez
Every bloom is you.

HE *sits, puts his head on* MISS CAKE *'s bosom and falls asleep.*

Following the JAILER's exit on page 263, and replacing dialogue
through the SERVANT's exit:

SERVANT   Goodnight.

MOTHER   Where are you going?

SERVANT   I don't know. Back to work perhaps.

MOTHER   Will you be all right?

SERVANT   Yes. Don't worry about me. I'll be all right. Good night.

105 and 106   Good night.

SERVANT   I'll see you.

105 and 106   Yes.

SERVANT   *(Sings)*

Listen . . . I feel . . .
I'll tell you in a moment . . . what I feel.
I have a thought somewhere in my head.
It's a fine thought. I'm sure it is.
It feels like a fine thought. Like a fine day.

And I know just what makes it fine.
Listen I feel, and I know just what I feel.
Listen, listen I feel. Listen I feel. Listen I feel.

SHE *exits*.

MARIA IRENE FORNES was born in Havana, Cuba, and emigrated to the United States with her family when she was fifteen. While studying painting in night school, she engaged in a variety of jobs, including typing, translating, and waiting on tables. After a brief term of study with Hans Hoffman at the Provincetown School, Miss Fornés went to Paris, where she lived for three years. In 1960, she started writing plays, which have since been presented all over Europe and the United States. Performances of her work have been given by Actors Workshop in San Francisco, the Firehouse Theatre in Minneapolis, and such noted New York groups as the Open Theatre, the Judson Poets Theatre, La MaMa Experimental Theatre Club, and the New Dramatists, as well as in such theatrical capitals as London, Amsterdam, Stockholm, and at the Festival of Two Worlds in Spoleto. She has received the Off-Broadway "Obie" Award for Distinguished Playwriting, and has been holder of a John Hay Whitney Fellowship, a Rockefeller grant from the Office of Advanced Drama Research in Minneapolis, a Yale-ABC Fellowship in Film Writing, and a residence fellowship of the Centro Mexicano de Escritores. The long-running Off-Broadway production of *Promenade* brought her extensive critical acclaim, and three of her other plays are scheduled to be produced Off-Broadway, including *Molly's Dream*, which Miss Fornés will direct herself. She is also a skilled designer, and has designed and executed costumes for many productions.